Rainwater Collection for the Mechanically Challenged

It was in the same part of Texas that a certain

rancher who was better at raising children than calves

went out one September night soon after dark and began

throwing handfuls of pebbles on the roof. His wife ran out

and asked him what in the world he meant.

"Well," he said, *"it's lightning in the west and*

might rain. This drouth has got to end sometime. That's

for certain. I thought it would be a good idear to kinder

break the kids into hearing something fall on the roof.

Then if it ever actually rains, they won't stampede."

—J.Frank Dobie, Tales of Old Time Texas

Dedicated to the

memory of Tré Arenz

1953-2003

RAINWATER
FOR THE MECHANIC

By Suzy Banks with Richard Heinichen
Illustrated by Tré Arenz

TANK TOWN PUBLISHING

COLLECTION
ALLY CHALLENGED

DRIPPING SPRINGS, TEXAS

www.rainwatercollection.com

We worked as hard as possible to get the information in this book
right, but since we're human and since change is the only constant,
you can't hold it against us if something's wrong. And at the risk of
sounding like your mother, do be careful when working on ladders
and around electricity.

Library of Congress Catalog Card Number: 2003096327

Banks, Suzy
Rainwater collection for the mechanically challenged/ written by
Suzy Banks and Richard Heinichen, illustrated by Tré Arenz.—2nd ed.

Includes bibliographical references and index.
ISBN 0-9664170-6-2

Book and Jacket Design by Drue Wagner and DJ Stout,
Pentagram Design, Austin, Texas / Trent Shepherd, Cold Shower
Design, Austin, Texas

Table of Contents

WE INITIALLY INSTALLED a rainwater system because our alternatives were bleak, bleak, bleak. Our new well, installed at a cost of around $5000, spewed rock hard, sulfur water that turned our hair into fright wigs and our blue jeans into cardboard. The idea of hooking up the two huge water softeners in tandem that we were told would be required to handle our water's extreme hardness and then feeding those monsters copious quantities of salt from now until the day we died was loathsome to us. Paying several thousand dollars to hook up to a private water supplier whose lines ran nearby and then paying hundreds of dollars a month for water until the day we died was equally abhorrent.

So we guttered our house and bought our first tank, foolishly believing we were "settling" for rainwater. Now, after years of living with "the gold standard"—water with a hardness of zero, that tastes fresh and leaves our faucets and tile sparkling—we realize no matter what conditions we had faced, choosing rainwater is not "settling" for less in any sense. Rainwater is, simply, the best. (It's so good that Richard started bottling it and selling it in 2002.)

We first put this book together back in 1997 as a beginner's guide to rainwater collection systems. We were beginners then. It is now 2003. We have weathered two serious droughts and have installed hundreds of rainwater collection systems. We have learned a lot more about rainwater collection and decided the time was ripe to update this little discourse.

We'll confess right up front that this book suffers the same major failing as a universal guide as its precursor did. Frankly, it's unabashedly regionally biased. We live in the Texas Hill Country outside of Austin. Our data about rainfall amounts, problems with incredibly hard water, and xeriscape recommendations are all gleaned from our tiny spot on the planet. Because we have no problems here (yet) with acid rain or serious industrial or agricultural air pollution, we skipped right over these concerns, which could be limiting factors in other parts of the country or the world when designing rainwater collection systems.

But what if you live in an area that receives much less rain than we do here? Frankly, we don't know if rainwater collection would be able to serve all your needs unless you were wildly conservative or you lived under a huge roof. But for anyone who sees an average of 30 inches or more of fairly clean rain annually and who has access to electricity in some form (supplied by the city, the sun, the wind or whatever), this book should see you well on your way to rainwater collection and self-sufficient nirvana.

There is one caveat to entering this nirvana, however. The privilege of independence comes with responsibility. This is your water supply. You are the sanitation engineer, the maintenance mechanic, the troubleshooting technician. You cannot point the finger at some hapless bureaucrat if you let your pipes freeze or you forget to change your filters or you don't keep your gutters clean or can't learn to conserve during dry spells. If you don't think rainwater and all its benefits—zero hardness without chemicals or salts, sparkling fixtures, cleaner clothes and bodies, longer lasting appliances, better tasting vegetables in your garden—are worth the effort, then shut this book right now and move back to the city where you can be mollycoddled, where all you have to do is turn on the faucet, pay the bill, and hope somebody somewhere keeps you supplied with water.

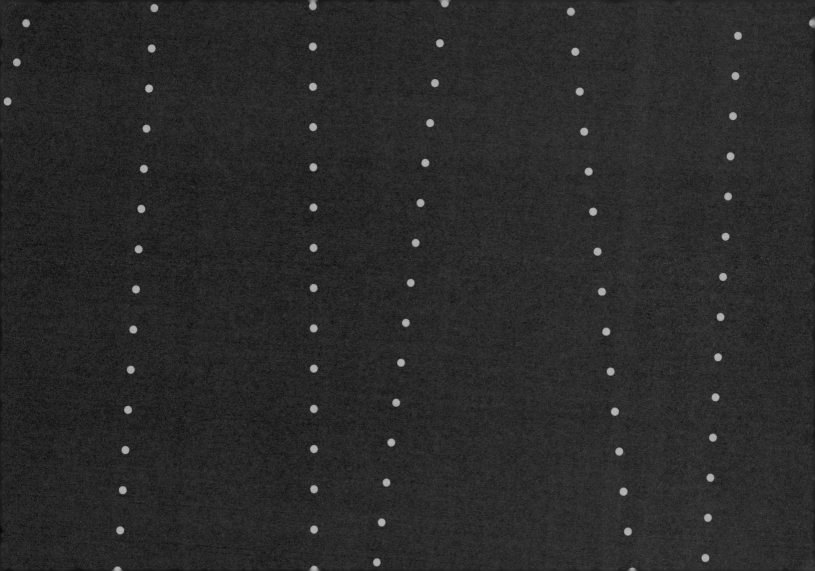

Chapter 1

A Day In the Life of a Raindrop

Chapter 1 A Day In the Life of a Raindrop

Remember the poster you made in elementary school of the hydrologic cycle? Well, it's one of the few things in the world that hasn't changed much since then.

Precipitation still falls from the sky, permeates through soil and runs off hard surfaces, collects in the ground, lakes, oceans and plants, then evaporates into the sky to begin its Sisyphean task again. In one year, 69,000 cubic miles of precipitation falls on the world's land masses.

All the water we use is captured at some stage of this cycle. (Okay, okay, so some miniscule percentage is created by chemical reactions or desalination...) Since water is considered a "universal solvent" in honor of its ability to dissolve some portion of nearly everything it touches, it makes sense to catch the rain before it has the chance to percolate through soil and rocks where it dissolves salts and minerals (not to mention contaminants like fecal coliform, pesticides, and chemicals). According to the Texas Water Development Board, "Rainwater quality almost always exceeds that of ground or surface water."

"Ah, but what about the air the rain falls through?" you ask. "What if it's polluted?" Well, first off, aren't you breathing that air? Seems like that should be your first concern. But, yes, rainwater can be contaminated by air pollution that plagues industrial areas, heavily populated cites, agricultural areas where crop dusting is common, and anywhere downwind from any of the sites mentioned above. And even in areas where falling rain is free of these hazards, your rainwater collection surface (i.e.: your roof) may also harbor contaminants like bacteria, molds, algae, bird poop, and squirrel pee. But what exactly do you think is in the raw source of many municipal water supplies? Austin, Texas, for example, taps Town Lake, a veritable stew of urban rubbish, for its water supply.

As for your own personal water supply, when collected rainwater is used solely for watering the yard, no treatment is required. To render rainwater potable, a series of filters and an ultraviolet light will do the trick. And for the truly persnickety or for kidney dialysis, nothing beats reverse osmosis, the same process a lot of those fancy bottled water companies use to turn tap water into "spring" water.

But please, let's not worry unnecessarily about killing cooties just yet. First, let's catch some rain.

The Hydrologic Cycle

Up on the roof top

And how are you going to catch that rain? For most household rainwater harvesting systems, the roof is the collection surface. Certainly, we have encountered a few people who insist on bucking this common sense approach, somehow convinced of the wisdom of collecting the water in tarps hung from trees or sheet steel propped against a hillside. But these are usually the same people who think seat belts are a government conspiracy or that a lack of a sense of humor is a sign of intelligence. So we suggest saving your imagination for more deserving pursuits and following the knowing herd on this one: collect the water off your roof.

What's the ideal roof surface?

Think smooth. We joke about the merits of glass roofs (stone-throwers aside), but when we stop laughing and get serious, we'd have to say the best roofs for rainwater collection are metal. If your existing roof isn't metal, don't despair. Unless it's flat and covered with tar and gravel (whoever invented this roof should be tarred and gravel-ed) or one of the old asbestos nightmares, nearly any roof can serve as a collection surface. It's not the particles, like those that might be washed off composition shingles, that present the biggest obstacle; those can easily be filtered out. Rather, it's the chemicals, like those used to treat wood shingles, that cause problems in water collected for potable use.

Fortunately, activated carbon filters in combination with ultraviolet light can remove nearly everything except radio-active particles and, most inconveniently, lead. And, also inconveniently, some old-time metal roofs, and even new roofs installed by old-time roofers, are attached using ring-shank nails outfitted with lovely lead washers. Also, on some roofs, lead "boots" are used as the flashing around plumbing vents. The solutions for the lead boots are simple: either replace them with the snappy new rubber boots or "seal" in the lead by painting the boots with latex paint. The solution for lead-washer screws is easy, too, but exceedingly tedious; replace the screws with new neoprene-washer screws.

A third option for getting the lead out is reverse osmosis, the ultimate water purification process. (But we're getting a little ahead of ourselves here. Filtration and disinfection will be covered ad nauseam in Chapter 5.)

How to Measure Square Footage of a Collection Surface

Measure at ground level below the edge of the roof. Don't measure along the slope of the roof.

A times B = collection area

How big should your roof be?

The square footage of your catchment surface is only as big as the footprint of your house—or your rain barn or your garage or whatever you've decided to use as your collection surface. "But wait!" you say. "I took geometry and I know that if my roof is sloped, the surface area is greater than the footprint of my house." Sure, sure. But the amount of rain that falls on the roof is not affected by the slope. (Really. Just trust us on this. And if you don't understand wait until you can't fall asleep some night to try to puzzle this out.) So when we talk about the size of your catchment surface, we're not talking about the square footage of your roof surface exactly, but about its useful dimensions as a collection surface.

Go Figure

Don't want to do the math? Can you at least read a chart?

Roof Size in Square Feet	Gallons per One Inch Rain	Gallons per 32 Inch Annual Rainfall
1000	550	17600
1100	605	19360
1200	660	21120
1300	715	22880
1400	770	24640
1500	825	26400
1600	880	28160
1700	935	29920
1800	990	31680
1900	1045	33440
2000	1100	35200
2100	1155	36960
2200	1210	38720
2300	1265	40480
2400	1320	42240
2500	1375	44000

A chunk of water that's one inch deep and one foot square equals exactly .6233 gallons. So, if one inch of rain falls on your 1000-square-foot roof, does this mean you'll collect 623.3 gallons? Ha! Don't you wish the real world worked like the laboratory! (Really, when's the last time you followed a cookie recipe precisely and came out with anywhere near the six dozen cookies it claimed to yield?) When counting up your raindrops, it's wise to err on the very conservative side. We figure at least as much as twenty percent of this perfect-world amount is lost due to evaporation, leaking and/or plugged gutters, blowing rain, sabotage by squirrels, and so on. So, we round the number down, down, down: In a one-inch rain, you'll collect about 550 gallons per 1000 square feet of collection surface.

Now that we've agreed on the numerical constant for our rainwater collection calculations, it's time to have some mathematical fun.

Remember all those story problems in elementary school, the ones about apples and pencils and party hats you said you'd never have any use for and so you slept through that section of math? Well, now you'll wish you'd stayed awake:

Let's say your house is 2300 square feet (because ours is). Let's say Austin (where we live) will actually get its average of 32 inches of rainfall this year. Your house is four miles from a major highway and is painted pink. (Remember how those sadist that wrote your math book used to throw those arbitrary facts in there?)

How much water can you collect in a year? (Big Hint: 2300 ÷ 1000 x 550 x 32=???) That's right! 40, 480! Now before you run out and apply for a job as a nuclear physicist, let's figure out how much water you'll use and how big your storage system should be.

How Much Do You Need?

A conserving household will use around 25 to 50 gallons per person. The two of us have averaged 26 gallons each a day for the last 98 days and we're not martyrs—honest, we take a shower every Saturday! (We couldn't do it alone. We must give credit to our very efficient toilets, fixtures, and appliances that we'll brag about later.)

Let's say there are four people in your household (won't that riffraff brother-in-law ever leave?) each using 30 gallons per day, for a total of 120 gallons per day. If we lived in Mawsynram, Meghalaya State, India, where the average annual rainfall is 467 inches a year, our collection tank would only have to be the size of a Big Gulp cup. But since we live in an area of biblical droughts, where rain hasn't fallen for as long as 75 days, we'll need storage to last us at least that long. Remember how we said to always err on the conservative side? Well, call us Cassandra (or Chicken Little: pick your myth), but we're going to bump that mind-frying drought up to 100 days without a drop of rain. We would have to store 12,000 gallons of water so Junior doesn't miss a bath and that brother-in-law has water to mix with his whiskey.

Now it's time to consider all four criteria: the size of your collection surface, the size of your collection tank, annual rainfall and your daily needs.

One woman we met—let's call her Optima—wanted to put in a 10,000-gallon collection tank. She calculated that she and her son would use 2000 gallons a month. But Optima only had a 900-square-foot collection surface. If we got 32 inches of rain, she would only collect 15,840 gallons (900 divided by 1000 times 550 times 32).

Something's got to give here. First, her collection tank is oversized for her collection surface. No matter how erratic the weather can get around here, we never get all our annual rainfall in a few weeks, like the Serengeti does. In the most general terms, we get a couple of inches each month and a little more in the fall and spring. Considering this steady precipitation and Optima's daily drain on her water supply, we'd wager the farm her tank would never be full and, worse, quite often empty. And her 24,000-gallon-a-year requirements will never be met, at least not during years with an average annual rainfall or less.

Optima is hoping to offset any shortfall by having water hauled in. While this can be a solution, it flies in the face of a sacred tenet of rainwater harvesting—independence. The water hauling company that's around one year may not be here the next and in times of severe drought, she might wait days and days before those busy water haulers will be able to deliver. If you plan on using supplemental water, first find out if such a service is available in your area. Thinking about hauling water yourself? Think first about the weight of water—over eight pounds a gallon. A 55-gallon drum weighs more than 440 pounds.

Optima would be better off trusting her water future to a rainbarn, a low-cost structure built to provide more collection surface. It also serves as a handy place to stash all that flotsam and jetsam that washes onto our personal shores as the years pass—bikes, broken lawnmowers, hoses, bird cages, scraps of wood.

A couple of years ago, we built a rainbarn that moonlights as a carport. At the risk of sounding like materialistic bores, we love it. It keeps our cars from exploding in the Texas summer sun and has added a huge hunk of pain-free catchment surface to our collection system. Have we confessed yet about how our house is a rainwater collector's nightmare, with weird and wacky rooflines overhung with lovely but messy oaks and cedar trees? Our rainbarn/carport boasts leaf-free gutters that drain immediately into the collection tank right beside it.

While a rainbarn might help Optima, it wasn't the solution for another homeowner we met. This fellow—let's call him Gluto—estimated the water needs of his family of five at 700 gallons a day! Seven hundred gallons! That's 255,500 gallons a year! Despite the fact that his collection surface topped 5000 square feet and despite the fact that he allowed for a storage capacity of 40,000 gallons, Gluto and his thirsty clan would not be able to survive on the 88,000 gallons he would collect during a year of average rainfall (32 inches). In fact, he wouldn't even come close to catching his required amount unless our area's annual precipitation tripled!

When we asked him if he'd considered conservation, he said he had to wash his car twice a week, take two showers a day, and bathe his horses every day. No matter how you juggle the numbers, no matter how many collection tanks he added or additional collection surfaces he built (short of a rainbarn the size of Vermont), it would be impossible to sate his gluttony.

In the *Texas Guide to Rainwater Harvesting*, elaborate worksheets help you calculate monthly water demand and storage capacity. But considering the vagaries of rainfall,

Simple is as simple does

This is the most basic worksheet to determine if rainwater harvesting is even a viable option for you:

1. Determine your total catchment area   _____ sq ft

2. Divide it by 1000. This equals   _____

3. Multiply by 550 to determine gallons collected per one inch of rain.   _____

4. Multiply this by the average annual rainfall in your area. In the monster state of Texas, land of deserts and swamps, this can range from 10 to 56 inches.   x _____ in

5. The amount of water you can probably collect is...   _____ gal

especially on a month-to-month basis, we think these worksheets are overly complex and too specific. Case in point: after a three-month drought in the spring of 2002, we received almost 20 inches of rain over a four-day period in July. We think it's best to think more in terms of average annual rainfall and plan accordingly. (The book, however, is a wealth of other wonderful rainy information. And, it's free!)

It's a good idea to plan for the worst while hoping for the best, so we recommend a safety margin like the one proposed by long-time rainwater user Mike McElveen: imagine you receive half your average rainfall and you use twice as much water as you think you do.

For us, that would mean a daily demand of 100 gallons for a total of 36,500 a year. If we only received 16 inches of rain a year, our collection surface would have to be 4000 square feet. If we added our 1440-square-foot barn and our new rainbarn/carport to the 2300-square-foot collection surface of our wacky house, we'd handily make it through the worst times imagined. And we have.

So, what did you come up with?

Do you think you can get by on that amount of water? For most people in this country, water is relatively cheap and pours into their lives with the flick of a faucet handle, so many are unaware of their water needs. Once you become a rainwater aficionado,

you'll become hyper-conscious of water consumption.

Of course, you probably already know the obvious water-saving techniques like not letting the water run while you brush your teeth. You also already know the benefits of installing low-flush toilets, those that use 1.6 gallons a flush rather than five or seven gallons like older models.

One extra long shower using 5 gallons per minute: 75 gallons

Hand-washing dishes throughout the day, water running: 25 gallons

Brushing teeth, water running at 2 gallons per minute (Don't forget to floss): 3 gallons

Washing Hands: 2.5 gallons

Flushing toilet: 1.5 gallons to 7 gallons (!) per flush

A Load of laundry in a top loading washer: 40-50 gallons

Dog Water Bowl: 2 quarts per day

These flushes add up. American Water Works Association, a nonprofit organization, estimates that low-flush toilets in every home could reduce water use by 3.5 billion gallons per day nationally. The city of Santa Fe, New Mexico, currently suffering from an extended drought and galloping water consumption, is so convinced of the potential water savings low-flushers provide that it recently budgeted $1.4 million to replace older, water-guzzling toilets throughout the city.

One of the biggest household water hogs is the washing machine. Top loading machines can use up to 50 gallons per load. But you don't have to run around in stinky, dirty clothes to skimp on wash water. Check out the front-loading or horizontal axis washing machines on the market. In 1995, when we bought our cute Swedish-built Asko, which uses a mere 17 gallons for a full-size load, most options for horizontal axis machines came with European pedigrees—Asko, Bosch, Miele, and so on—as well as European price tags. (Our Asko was nearly 1500 bucks.)

Now, many US appliance manufactures—Maytag, GE and others—are breeding their own water-efficient washing machines and the prices are a mite easier to stomach. And front-loading washing machines offer other benefits as well. They get wash loads cleaner using less detergent with less wear and tear on the clothes. They spin more water out of the laundry, reducing drying time. And according to the EPA, they use 50 percent less energy than conventional washers. (And honest, we don't own stock in Universal Horizontal-Axis Washing Machine Oligopoly, Inc.)

Landscape Considerations

During the summer months, one-quarter to one-half of municipal water used goes to maintain water-guzzling residential landscapes. A half-inch of water sprinkled on a 1000-square-foot lawn will suck about 300 gallons of water out of your system. St. Augustine lawns require at least 50 inches of rain a year, much more than our area's average rainfall. So that same 1000-square-foot yard will require 18 supplemental inches of water for a total of at least 9600 gallons! And don't even think about the water your lawn will demand during a drought! If you're going to collect rain as your sole source of water, it's time to rethink that St. Augustine lawn and those lovely, thirsty begonias.

Xeriscaping, which uses regionally-adapted and drought tolerant plants, is your solution. Native plants are the figures in your formula. And if you think you're limited to a couple of yuccas and some concrete statuary, you should take a look at the grounds at the National Wildflower Research Center outside Austin, especially the demonstration gardens which compare water-usage of native landscapes—both "naturalized" and formal—

with the traditional canna-St. Augustine-red-tipped-photinia yard.

While supplemental watering is occasionally needed in some areas at the center, especially during serious droughts, the landscaping here should be all you need to see to convince you of the beautiful possibilities of xeriscaping. (Be sure to check out their 70,000-gallon rainwater collection system.) If you live in Texas, you should also take a look at Sally and Andy Wasowski's *Native Texas Plants, Landscaping Region by Region* for inspirational garden designs. There are similar books available for other regions of the country.

If you do need to water your landscape, think about installing a drip irrigation system that uses 60 percent less water than conventional, wasteful sprinklers. Or you might want to consider a greywater irrigation system that reuses the waste water from your home—everything except the toilets and the kitchen sink—to water the garden.

Chapter 2

The Storage Tank

The Barrel
Price Tag: free to $100
Size: 55 gallons to 100 gallons

For a small system—really not a system at all, but a bucket-stuck-under-a-downspout to collect rainwater for those persnickety African violets—all you'll need is a 55-gallon drum. Make sure it didn't contain anything toxic in its past life. (We're particularly fond of the ones that contained chocolate syrup.) For something a little more decorative, try a wooden whiskey barrel.

And please, think about mosquitoes. Just covering the barrel may not inhibit the little buggers from breeding if they can fly in and out via the downspout. You may need to screen the top of the downspout or the inlet of the barrel to deter these bloodsuckers.

While collecting rainwater in a barrel is simple enough, getting the water out of the barrel to your plants is a

> We use fiberglass tanks and we primarily sell fiberglass tanks. With that admission we will try to give an unbiased review of the variety of tanks available for storage.

Plastic Rainbarrel

smidgen trickier. Options include ladling it out (how tedious); siphoning it out the top; attaching a spigot at the bottom of the tank using a bulkhead fitting; or pumping the water out using a submersible pump or a jet pump. If you decide to gravity feed the water from the barrel to the flower bed, be forewarned about the mysterious phenomena known as friction or head loss.

Stone
Price Tag: an arm and a leg
    per gallon
Size: 2000 gallons to
Whatever You Can Afford

New Stone Cistern

Oh, yes. Wouldn't we all love to live in a restored 1850s farmhouse with a functioning cistern of cut limestone? But unless you're a master mason, have won the lottery, or can blackmail one of the few remaining stone craftsmen into building you a stone tank, you can count on spending Junior's university tuition on this. (And we're not talking the local community college, here.)

In addition to its high price, a stone cistern is more difficult to maintain than a monolithic tank. For a potable water supply, it must be constructed using non-toxic materials or it must be fitted with a potable-approved liner that can cost as much as a dollar a square foot.

The Texas Hill Country is dotted with lovely old stone cisterns, some still in use. If nothing else, their presence speaks to the endurance of the tradition of rainwater collection for a household water supply.

Concrete or Ferro-Cement
Price Tag: 35 cents to $1 per gallon
Size: 10,000 gallons and up, up, up.

Ferro-cement construction uses multiple layers of wire lathe or chicken wire shaped around a steel framework. Concrete tanks

Old Dog with Old Stone Cistern

are usually poured in place. In new construction they can often be handily integrated into the design of the house to serve dual purposes: storage tank and patio or skating rink. Only the available space and your budget limit the size. These tanks can be constructed above or below ground, and are an owner-built option only for someone very handy and very hardworking.

While there is a risk of cracking and leaking, especially in underground tanks in expansive clay soils, repairs can be made fairly easily, although the tank may have to be drained to make the repairs. (There are some pastes like Waterplug that can be applied underwater but we're uncertain about their effect on potable water quality.) The biggest drawback for concrete or ferro-cement tanks for people like us—who don't plan well and love to change their minds—is their

irrefutably permanent placement. For others, this may actually be a plus.

It's worth noting that more than a few people with concrete or ferro-cement tanks have complained to us about the smell and taste of their water. Making certain that the tanks are plastered with high-quality potable-approved material is paramount for a happy life with ferro-cement and concrete. Some people have been forced to retrofit their tanks with expensive plastic liners, a task that's much trickier than it sounds.

Another concrete option is a ready-made tank. Some come as stacking rings that are sealed together, a sort of variation on the constructed-in-place tank. Other tanks, both cylindrical and rectangular, are completely fabricated off site and dropped into place. The benefit of these tanks is their sturdiness, their long lives, and the fact they can be buried partially or completely.

Concrete Rings, Ferro-Cement

Old Metal, New Metal

Metal
Price Tag: 40 to 60 cents per gallon without liner
Size: 200-2000 gallons

Metal tanks have an undeniable retro appeal unmatched by any other material except stone. They are lightweight and easily transported. We have an older metal tank we use for collecting water only for our garden since we're not sure whether lead was used in its soldered joints or not. It's cute, but it's rusting like crazy. Also, pH "bounce" can cause zinc to be leached into the water. (The universal solvent, remember?) However, manufacturers of newer galvanized tanks, especially those constructed expressly for rainwater collection, avoid these potential problems by treating the bottom with a special coating to inhibit corrosion and coating the inside of the tank with a potable-approved liner that prevents rusting and corrosion.

Polypropylene
Price Tag: 35 to $1 per gallon
Size: 300 gallons to 10,000 gallons

Poly Tanks

We had a polypropylene (or poly) tank that we used as a pump tank to hold and transfer the water collected from one side of our wacky house to our main storage tanks. We bought it in Nuevo Laredo, Mexico, for cheap, cheap. So if you're headed that way to do a little border shopping you can pick one up, too. They carry them at all the hardware stores down there. We paid about 900 pesos ($120) for a potable-approved 1100 liter/290-gallon tank with a lid.

Not headed to Mexico? Many farm and ranch supply stores in the U.S stock a wide variety of the sturdy, lightweight fellows. Just be sure that you get a completely opaque tank (which typically means a black tank). If you get a clear or translucent tank like one man we knew – let's call him Oblivio – you will be growing more slimy algae in it than in a long-neglected aquarium.

While ever-popular poly tanks—cheap, long-lasting, lightweight, and widely available— have much to commend them, they aren't without their faults. First off, at the risk of sounding shallow, we think they're undeniably homely. And you can't paint them. Also, if a pitch black tank is baking out in the sun, the water can't help but heat up. When considering a poly tank,

Round Cistern Capacity in Gallons

Depth	Diameter in feet				
	5	10	12	14	16
5'	735	2935	4230	5755	7515
8'	1176	4696	6768	9208	12024
10'	1470	5870	8460	11510	15030
12'	1764	7044	10152	13812	18036

think about what we call the Mass Factor: the greater the volume of water in the tank, the cooler it will stay. And cool is good. At least here in Texas. (In defense of poly tanks, we've heard only one complaint—and a dubious one at that—about a plastic or "off" taste and smell in the water.)

Another snag with poly tanks is that the fittings aren't an integral part of the tank itself. To attach trunk lines or suction lines you have to drill holes in the tanks and attach fittings called bulkhead fittings. These "after-manufacture" fittings don't always leak, but they do so more than anyone wants them to.

capacity, pump all the water into one tank while we cleaned the other, and not lose a drop of water. Plus, they keep each other company. Plus, we didn't have enough money for one big tank back then.

The tanks we sell and use have an interior coating of FDA-approved food-grade resin. The exterior, a UV resist-ant gel-coat, is completely opaque to inhibit algae growth. These tanks, which are used in many commercial situations such as oil fields, have weath-ered the elements for decades without deterioration. If a fiberglass tank should become damaged, like if your militia

Fiberglass Tanks

Fiberglass

Price Tag: 38 cents to
    1.50 per gallon
Size: 2000-57,000

We have two 4000-gallon fiberglass tanks for our house-hold use. Even though one 8000-gallon tank would have been cheaper per gallon, we like the versatility of two tanks; if one should be damaged by a meteorite or something, we could still use the second tank while the other is being repaired. Or say we need to clean them. We could wait until we're at half-storage

Duck Fiberglass Tank

crazed neighbor takes a few pot shots at it, it can be easily repaired.

Another bonus to fiberglass tanks is that they can be painted with plain old latex house paint. You can paint them to camouflage them or celebrate them. Out at Tank Town, our rainwater collection store, we have a whole herd of tanks painted in eye-popping colors Martha Stewart might have picked. Artist friends have used a few as canvases, covering one with yellow duckies and transforming a couple of short, squatty tanks into a sea turtle and a ladybug. Who says you can't have fun with this?

Turtle tank painted by Celia Berry

Turtle fiberglass tank

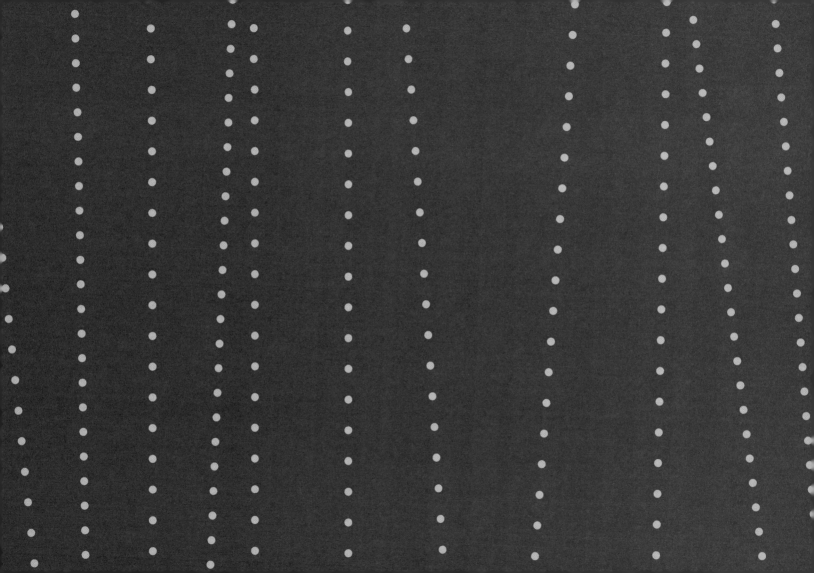

Chapter 3

Siting Your Tank

RALPH WALDO EMERSON must have been talking about rainwater collection systems when he said, "To be simple is to be great." The fewer pumps, the fewer twists and turns in your pipe, and the more straightforward your design, the less you'll have to hassle with maintenance.

In a perfect world, you'd have a huge rainbarn and cisterns on top of a hill nearly a hundred feet higher in elevation than your house. At this height, gravity alone would supply you with water pressure around 40 psi—a municipal standard. You wouldn't have to worry about pump failure or power outages, at least not until you woke up from your dream world and joined us back in Reality Land. Here, nearly all us mere mortals on subdivision lots or small acreage rely on pumps, as in "the water runs off the roof, into gutters and into the collection tank where it is then pumped to the house/ pressure tank/hippo habitat."

> Water gains one pound per square inch of water pressure for every 2.31 feet of rise or lift. Say you want pressure of 40 psi at your house. How high would the collection tank have to be above your house to supply this kind of pressure using gravity alone? 2.31 feet of lift x 40 psi= 92.4 feet.

The Tank

Even if Mr. Gravity won't work solo in your situation, he can at least assist your pump if you place your tank at the highest workable level. But the inlet on your tank should be lower, of course, than the lowest downspout on your gutters and, actually, to adjust for any friction loss in the trunkline, a couple of feet lower than the lowest downspout if possible.

When locating your tank, you should also consider the mortifying prospect that you may run out of rainwater because of a record breaking drought or wanton overuse and will have to call in a water truck for a supplemental supply. (This has never happened to us, despite the drought of '96.) Think too about placing your tank where it can be shaded and camouflaged by trees.

If you're converting from well water to a rainwater system, putting your tanks near your well house gives you the option of using your existing plumbing with the least amount of hassle. And an underground tank, especially, should be at least fifty feet away from a septic field.

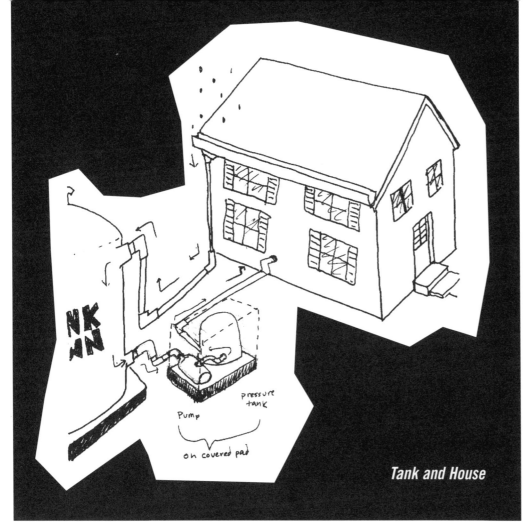

Pump

pressure tank

on covered pad

Tank and House

She Ain't Heavy, She's my Cistern

Since water weighs about eight pounds per gallon, a 5000-gallon tank of water will tip the scales at 40,000 pounds. For an above ground tank, this mammoth tonnage requires a stable, level pad. Surprisingly, many people assume stable and flat means complicated and expensive. They build concrete footings and haul in fill and rubble like they're constructing a freeway overpass in earthquake country. Don't do this; it's overkill and we will make fun of you if you do. If your chosen site is level, with no rocks bigger than a golf ball or tree roots bigger than a pencil, on a bed of cushion-y pea gravel or a bed of caliche that's well compacted, you may not have to do a thing besides point the tank delivery truck in the right direction. Most everyone else, besides cliff dwellers, can use a simple pad like the one shown here. Do keep in mind the considerable weight of water; a 10,000-gallon tank when full will weigh over 80,000 pounds. A tree stump protruding in your pad can crack the bottom of your full tank like a bullet through safety glass.

Crash Pad

Get four 2x4s of the appropriate length to accommodate the diameter of your tank. (Hint: Tank is ten foot in diameter? Use ten foot boards.) Nail them together flat, not on edge.

If toe-nailing them together is too big a chore, attach the boards using metal angle plates or a thin short board as a sort of splint.

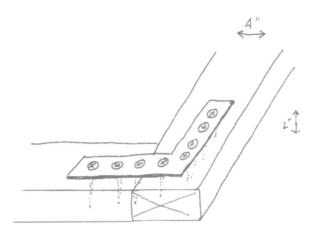

4"

2"

Fill the square with small particle material and screed it off. We especially like road base because it's cheap and compacts nicely if you do a vigorous stomp-dance on it. (Recommended tunes: Happy Feet by 8 ½ Souvenirs or Viva Las Vegas by Elvis.) Sprinkle the whole pad with a bag of Portland cement, rake in, and dampen with water or just let it harden naturally like all those solidified bags of concrete in your garage that sucked moisture right out of the air.

Level the frame by shimming with debris or rocks or pieces of all those plastic toys lying around the yard you swore you'd never buy your kid. If you have to raise any corner higher than half a foot, you may want to secure your handiwork by mixing up some cement and tossing a few shovels full onto the rocks or debris you used.

If you MUST have a pump tank...

Pump Tank

The Pump Tank

In some systems, especially those retrofitted to existing houses, the rainwater can't be collected directly into the main storage tank. We can blame gravity, aesthetics, deed restrictions, uncooperative elevations or any combination of these for this snafu. In these cases, there's no getting around the less-than-perfect pump tank. A pump tank, which is sometimes called a surge tank just to keep things confusing, is a small-ish tank that's paired with a powerful pump—either a submersible pump or an external pump fitted to the side of the tank. The pump tank's sole purpose in life is to collect and quickly divert rainwater to the main storage tank.

The reason this isn't an ideal system is because of Murphy and his multiple laws. In the case of pump tanks, this law reads: The more desperately you need the rainwater, the more likely a lightning bolt will knock out your power during that great, first thunderstorm of the spring, incapacitating the pump in your pump tank and your ability to collect all or—gasp!—any of the water gushing off your roof and into your gutters.

You'll be much happier with your less-than-ideal pump tank if you make sure to size the pump properly by determining the maximum amount of water per hour it will be required to pump during the ultimate frog-strangling gully-washer.

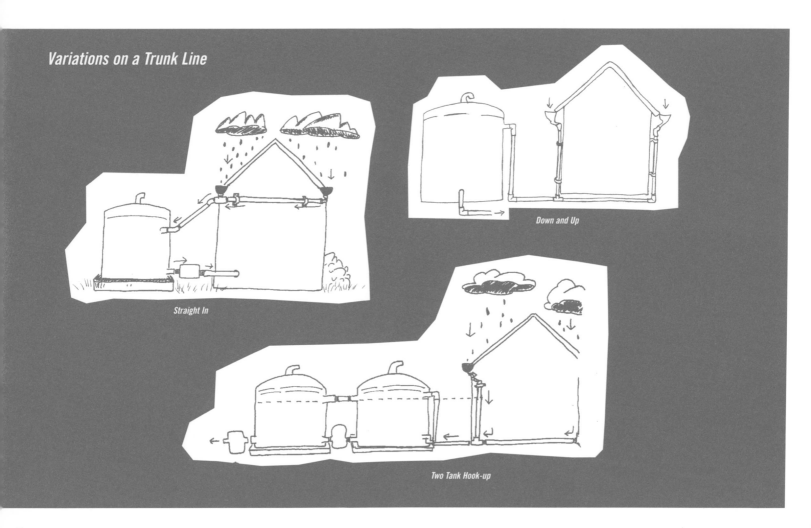

Variations on a Trunk Line

Straight In

Down and Up

Two Tank Hook-up

36

Rain in the Fast Lane

According to the Rainfall Frequency Atlas of the United States, the hundred-year maximum rainfall rate per hour in Travis County, Texas is 4.3 inches! If it's coming down this fast, you may be too busy inflating your personal flotation device to worry about water collection. Fortunately for your pump, a more typical maximum around Austin—and the rest of the country, for that matter—in any certain year is 1.6 inches per hour. You might want to consider that you may receive half of that 1.6 inches in ten minutes or less and size your system components accordingly.

How does this translate into pumping capacity?

Well, let's take our 2300-square-foot collection surface and hit it with 1.6 inches in an hour. In this scenario, let's pessimistically say every drop of the water from your roof collects in an auxiliary pump tank and is then transferred to your main collection tanks.

Our formula is: 2300 ÷ 1000 x 550 x 1.6 =

Click, click, click on your calculator and you should come up with a total of 2024 gallons in one hour. Reasonably priced submersible and shallow well jet pumps are available that can handle this volume.

But what about Murphy's preordained power failure during this deluge? There are solar pumps and low-voltage pumps that operate off a deep cell battery, but the affordable ones (around $150 for a Shurflow low-voltage to $745 for the top-of-the-line solar Slowpump) only handle 150 to 240 gallons per hour. A more practical solution might be to size your pump tank as large as possible so that it can serve as a small storage tank in a power outage and calculating your needs knowing that there may be times when you just can't catch it all.

Voice of Experience

Dr. Mike McElveen and his family are rainwater harvesting heroes around these parts. They started collecting rainwater back in 1983 because they were concerned about the calcium scale developing around the rim of their potted plants. They noticed how much better their plants began to do once they were watered with rainwater rather than well water and the McElveens began to wonder if they themselves might do better on rainwater. Their system, as well as the collection systems of two other modern day rainwater pioneers, is explored on a 30-minute video, Rainwater Collection Systems. This guide to rainwater collection is a great introduction for anyone considering "the gold standard" for a water supply. It's available through Gardening Naturally Productions.

Chapter 4

The Buddy System

Getting the Water Into Your Tank

Gutters

Price Tag: 30 cents a linear foot for do-it-yourself vinyl or
  plastic up to $15 per foot for copper installed by pros

For something with such a simple name and basic function, gutters are more complicated than they might appear at first glance. One do-it-yourself book rates installing gutters and downspouts as a "five" on a difficulty scale of one to ten. The skills don't take years to master; it's just such picky, precise work done while balancing at the top of an extension ladder wishing you'd hired someone besides that drunken brother-in-law to help.

Hung improperly, gutters can look awful, rot out your facia board (the piece of lumber attached to the end of your rafters), breed mosquitoes and, worst of all, fail to capture all the water running off your roof. So, do it right.

In the dark ages, gutters were made of wood and, for the feudal lord's castle, copper. Today's cutting edge materials include: 1) galvanized steel, sometimes fashioned into dapper, flow-efficient

Tanks and roofs alone don't make your system fly. In most instances, you can't get by without:

- Gutters
- Pipes to carry the water to and from the tank
- A pump and a pressure tank
- Electricity, solar panels, or (yikes!) a hand pump

And you're going to want:

- A roof washer or some pre-collection filtration
- Sediment filter
- Activated charcoal filter
- UV light or ozone generator
- Maybe, if you're picky, point-of-use reverse osmosis filtration

half-round shapes; 2) aluminum, the seamless variety of which must be professionally installed for the price of a midsize sedan ($3.50/foot); 3) cheap plastic, that looks and behaves like cheap plastic, leaking, breaking and warping; and 4) vinyl, good for the do-it-yourselfer because the components are "welded" together with vinyl cement and attach easily to any PVC trunk lines snaking around the house.

In the Beginning, There Were Numbers

Measure the length of your eaves to determine how many gutter sections—typically ten feet long—you'll need. You'll need one downspout for every 40 to 50 feet of straight gutter run. This may mean you'll have to have one or more center drops on an especially long run. (A center drop is a downspout not located at the end of a gutter run, but rather somewhere in the "center." Get it? One center drop with a three-inch hole can handle the run off from 700 square feet of surface area.)

Count up your downspouts. To determine how many elbows—typically 75-degree bends—that you'll need, double the number of downspouts. (One elbow will make the turn from the roof overhang towards the wall and a second elbow will then make the turn against the side of the house.)

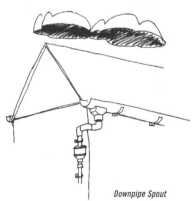

Downpipe Spout

Downpipes, sometimes called leaders or even downspout pipes by more literal-minded folks, also come in ten-foot lengths; you'll need at least one for every downspout, more if you're guttering a multi-level house, less if your

PVC piping extends higher up the wall to meet the downpipe. (Note: Downpipe cannot be glued together so that it can hold standing water. PVC pipe can be. You will have to run the PVC pipe at least a little higher—something like two feet higher—than the inlet of your tank.)

You'll need a bracket at least every 30 inches along your facia board or one on each rafter end. You'll also need to add up how many downpipe straps, 90- and 45-degree inside or outside corners, end caps, and downpipe connectors to order.

Many types of gutters come with directions specific to their installation—particulars about brackets, straps and spikes and connecting the sections. One gutter rule, however, is universal:

For every ten-foot run, gutters should drop towards the downspout $1/4$- to $1/2$-inch. (Can't those experts agree on anything?)

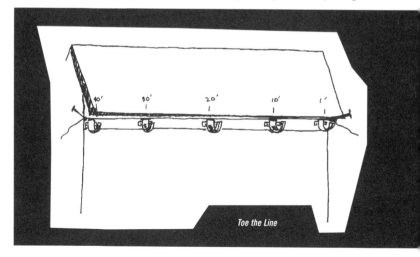

Toe the Line

Shooting the Slope

At one end of your run, at the point where the highest bracket will go, tap a nail into your facia board or rafter end as high as a bracket will comfortably fit, typically right under the roof edge. At the other end of your run, where the downspout will go, measure down one inch from the roof edge, then tap in a little nail at that spot. Stretch a string between these two nails to mark the gentle, but crucial slope that will be your guide to attaching the middle brackets.

Gutter Hygiene

We discuss post-collection filtration and disinfection in Chapter 5. But your first line of defense is right here, literally in the gutter, where you must battle to limit as much organic matter as possible from even reaching your tank.

Like the aging, tree-hugging hippies we are, we tucked our house into a grove of old growth cedars, scrub oaks and live oaks, some growing mere centimeters from our stucco walls. Unlike many new homes, ours looks like it belongs here or, at least, has been here long enough it doesn't matter anymore whether it belongs or not. The trees shade our roof and are the playground of rich and famous squirrels, birds, and other lively creatures who feed on the acorns and juniper berries. But there is a dark side to this Disney-esque scenario in the form of leaves, twigs, pollen and poop. Keeping this discharge out of our gutters and out of our tanks is a constant challenge, a challenge compounded by the rambling design of our house, with its multiple levels and numerous downspouts.

Fortunately, others have faced the same challenge and many products are out there to assist in the task:

Don't eyeball this slope. Measure the run, which is the distance along your roof edge where the gutters will hang, and round up to the nearest ten-foot increment. Say you have a 38-foot run. With a 1/4 inch drop every ten feet, you'll need around an inch of drop. (40 ÷ 10 x 1/4 = 1 inch.) If your gutters are destined to accumulate more than the most minimal amounts of leaves and debris, you'd best hang them with a bit more slope to keep the debris from inhibiting the flow of water.

Leaf guards

These run along the top of the gutters and ostensibly keep the gutters free of leaves. They didn't work for us. Maybe they're designed for regions of the country where all the leaves are big, like maple leaves, and the pollen sacks are large, hard pods. Here in the Texas Hill Country, where our beloved live oaks taunt us each spring with a pollen drop reminiscent of a nuclear fallout, this gritty and abundant mess slips right through the grid of the leaf guard and accumulates like sludge in the gutter. Cleaning the gutters became an incredible chore since we had to remove the guard each time to get at the oak gunk and the juniper berries from the cedar trees.

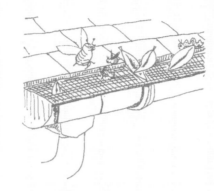

Strainer baskets

These spherical leaf guards sit in the exit hole of the downspout. Once again, a great gizmo for keeping the big stuff out of your water supply, but of no use against smaller tree debris. We tried tubes of insect screen inserted vertically into the downspout, but we soon discovered these screens worked better lying flat across the downspout hole, with the ends of the screen securely tucked under the gutter. Each time we clean out the gutters—usually in the middle of a thunderstorm at midnight—we shake all the flotsam and jetsam out of the little pieces of screen and tuck them back in. Crude but relatively effective. We've also used hardware cloth, the 1/4-inch grid size. While certainly not as fine a filter as the insect screen, it doesn't clog as easily either.

Funnel Fun

If the inlet of your collection tank is several feet lower than the top of your downpipe, instead of climbing up to the leaf strainers, you may be able to bring them down to your level by inserting a galvanized funnel, fitted with a brass screen, into your downpipes. Cut the leaf strainer in at shoulder height or as low as the highest standing water in your downpipes will allow. Make sure the upper portion of the downpipe doesn't extend into the funnel too far or the debris might back up into the downpipe, plug it, and defeat the fun of the funnels. Simply clean out the funnel while standing flat-footed on terra firma wearing your Sunday best.

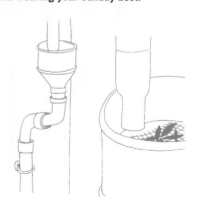

Gutter to Tank

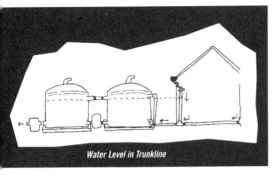

Water Level in Trunkline

The pipe run from your downspout(s) to the tank is no place to suddenly become stingy. For a 3000-to 5000-square-foot collection surface, a three-inch diameter downpipe for every 50 feet of gutter run or for every 700 square feet of collection surface, tied into a four-inch diameter PVC trunkline running to the collection tank, should do the trick. For smaller collection surfaces, two-inch diameter downspouts every 40 feet of gutter run, tied into a three-inch PVC trunkline line works great.

And just because you're being practical, there's no reason to abandon aesthetics. The pipe from your downspout to your tank doesn't have to run through the air. Let it snuggle up to the side of the house, run along the ground and then back up to the inlet on the tank. Really, this will work. The Egyptian water level is based on this principal, where water always seeks equal level. Some people, however, have a hard time understanding this concept. But as long as the inlet on the tank is lower than your lowest downspout, the rain will flow into your tank. (Okay, so the inlet might actually need to be a couple of feet lower than your lowest downspout to account for any friction loss over the length of the trunkline, but you get the picture.) The trunkline and downpipes simply remain filled with water to a height level with the inlet of your tank.

Roof Washer

No matter how diligent you are on a "gutter-al" level, some amount of debris is going to slip by. Your second line of defense for keeping these foreign bodies out of your storage tank is a roof washer, a device for either filtering, diverting, or capturing the first, dirtiest wash of water that flows off your roof at the beginning of a rain event.

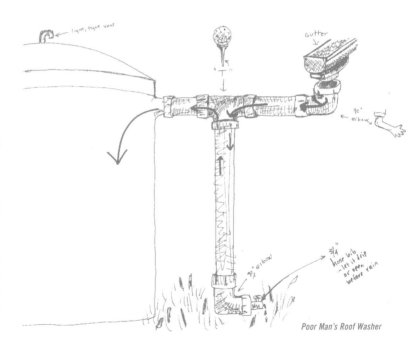

Poor Man's Roof Washer

Poor Man's Roof Washer
Price Tag: around $25 in PVC parts

In our early days as neophyte rainwater farmers, our system was outfitted with what we call the Poor Man's Roof Washer. Right before the collected water shot into the inlet on our tank, the first flush off the roof—the water carrying all the leaves and stuff—was diverted into a three-inch PVC pipe running to the ground with a cleanout fitting on the bottom. Once the tube was filled, the rest of the captured rain flowed into the tank. We thought this was a pretty nifty way to keep the dirtiest water—the first to run off our roof after a dry spell—out of our tanks. And it was.

Sort of.

First off, we had a problem with some debris in the tube floating to the top of the tube and then into the tank. But this isn't the worst hitch in this program. The real trouble starts when you neglect to drain the pipe after a rain and the water inside freezes and cracks the PVC elbow at the bottom, a crack you don't notice until the next big rain when the whole mess sort of blows off the bottom of the pipe and all that precious rainwater goes shooting down on the ground instead of into your half-full tanks. Very depressing. Especially since it's a true story that happened to us.

Not nearly as depressing, however, as what might occur with a system using a manual diversion valve, a device mentioned, but seldom recommended in any of the books we've read about water systems. The major drawbacks of this type of roof washer are human forgetfulness and the fact that rain doesn't always fall at the most convenient times. If you're asleep or at work when

the valve needs to be turned, you'll either collect the dirty water in your cistern or lose all the rain.

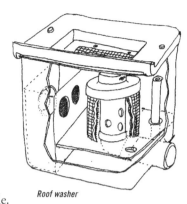

Roof washer

A Manufactured Roof Washer
Price Tag: $400-800

More effective, but often more maintenance-demanding roof washers are commercially available. One made by Water Filtration Company is like a giant fiberglass shoebox fitted with a filter or filters. As the rainwater passes through the filters, they remove anything bigger than 60 microns. Several years ago we installed one of these gizmos and now know the rigorous attention to cleanliness these filters require.

If you neglect them, they can become a source of contamination rather than a defense against it. We've also learned you've got to keep the filter clean or it will restrict the flow of rainwater significantly, so much so that the rainwater will be trickling into your tank while it gushes out the top of the roof washer or out of the tops of your downspouts during a downpour.

We have received calls from more people than we care to remember who are convinced they have a break or a plug in the trunkline. "It's been raining and we aren't collecting any water!" they yell. When we stop by the scene of the crime, we first check to see how packed their gutters are. Then we take a gander at their roof washer filter. Sometimes you can't even tell it's a filter at all; it looks more like a solid, compacted cylinder of mud, ancient

Roof washer on wood stand

Roof washer on metal stand

The Eliminator: The Ferrari of Roof Washers
Price Tag: $875

Okay, we admit it. No matter how hard we tried to apply pop-Zen philosophy to cleaning the roof washer filter, we never mellowed to the task. We were always stewing about a better, slicker way to capture the first flush rather than filter it. The product of all this mental stewing is our new invention: the Eliminator. This simple, but hard-working fellow eliminates the need for a pre-storage filter; it eliminates the time it takes to clean that filter; and it eliminates the accumulation of organic gunk in your storage tank.

Instead of relying on filtration, the Eliminator captures a metered wash of rainwater—the first, dirtiest wash—before it can enter the storage tank. Because we realize that water, especially rainwater, is precious, the amount of water you capture in the Eliminator is adjustable. This amount is individually determined by your particular system's conditions: the size of the collection surface, the amount of organic debris (i.e. a lot of trees overhanging the collection surface) it's subjected to, and even seasonal variables (i.e. pollen season vs. pollen-free season).

The total capacity of the Eliminator is 275 gallons, a sufficient first wash amount for a 4000-square-foot house. The first time you use the Eliminator, it will fill completely before the rainwater is diverted into the main collection tank. Before the next rain event, you drain the Eliminator to your appropriate level. For this task, there's a ball valve at the bottom of the unit and a site indicator marked in 25-gallon increments along the side. During the next rain event, only the designated amount of water will be captured in the Eliminator.

algae, and mysterious space dust, with some dead beetles encased in it for good measure. When we show the homeowners the filter, they are typically shocked, slightly belligerent, and then completely repentant.

So, despite the fact it will never be anyone's favorite chore, cleaning the roof washer filter cannot be ignored. And how often should you clean it? After every substantial rain. (Not every couple of years as one homeowner thought.) Cleaning the filter is not fun, but rather than looking at it as an odious nuisance, why not think of it as a repetitive activity that grounds you? No? Okay, you can at least make this dirty task a little easier by buying an extra filter. That way you'll always have a clean filter on hand, in theory, anyway. Take the encrusted one to the car wash for a high-pressure bath.

We recommend capturing 75 gallons per thousand square feet of roof surface for optimum cleaning of a roof burdened with lots of organic matter down to 25 gallons per thousand square feet for a system that's unaffected by overhanging trees and such. It might take a little experimentation to determine the amount of water you should capture for your particular situation. If you have lots of standing water in your trunk line that you typically drain between rain events (to protect against freezing or to combat mosquito breeding), this might reduce the amount of water the Eliminator needs to capture. Also, if it hasn't rained in some time, you may need to capture more water than if it's been raining for a couple of days already and you know your roof and gutters are already as clean as they'll ever be.

Eliminator Valve

Eliminator

About the only maintenance the Eliminator requires is the dumping of a designated amount of captured water between rain events so the Eliminator will be set to collect the next dirty flush of rainwater. (You have to drain water out to let more dirty water in.) Seasonally, you may want to drain the Eliminator completely to nip mosquito breeding in the bud. (Don't fret: You don't have to waste all this precious water, only divert it onto your flower patch.) If you open the two-inch ball valve all the way when there's a substantial amount of water in the Eliminator, this should be all you need to do to flush out any settled debris. But there's also a handy four-inch cleanout on the bottom so that, if you must, you can reach in and remove big clumps of stuff or hose the Eliminator out a couple of times a year.

Post Filtering With Big Sandy
Price Tag: $150-$500

Now, if even the Eliminator sounds like a hassle, there's an even more effortless way to keep—or rather get—your stored water spanking clean. In this scenario, you let all the junk flow unimpeded into your tank. That's right, let it all flow in. You're not worried because you're going to remove it by circulating it through a sand filter that extracts anything larger than 24 microns. These are the exact sand filters used to clean swimming pool water.

Using a pump, you suck the water from an outlet on the bottom of your collection tank, circulate it through the sand filter, and then discharge the clean water back into another inlet on the bottom of the tank. (Why should both the inlet and outlet be on the bottom of your tank? It helps to stir up the debris that settles there.)

For the sand filter to work well, you've got to spring for the biggest one you can afford. A rinky-dink sand filter befitting a hot tub, for instance, will be exhausted in a day by the task at hand. And definitely do not use a pleated filter system. Those pleated filters are astronomically expensive to replace, they can be ruined during cleaning, and you can waste a load of water trying to clean them. Also, while it may be tempting to circulate the water using a timer, this isn't very efficient. If weeks or even months pass between rain events, you'll be wasting energy to filter water that's already clean. It's best to visually inspect your water to decide when it's time to filter it.

A nifty trick: If you want to see how clean or dirty the water in your collection tank is, simply tie a nice, white PVC fitting, like a two-inch coupling, onto the end of a string, and lower it through the tank manway to the bottom of the tank. (You can feel the reverberations through the string when the PVC fitting hits the bottom of the tank.) If you can see the fitting, glowing white back at you, then the water is clean. If it's obscured in a cloud or, worse, completely hidden, you know it's time for some filtration.

The advantage of this post-collection filtration technique is the little maintenance it requires. All you'll ever have to do is backwash the filter (no more complicated than turning a valve on for a few minutes and turning it off). Amazingly, you never have to replace the sand. The suspended solids you see in the water when you backwash aren't sand; it's the gunk you filtered out.

The disadvantage of this setup is that sand filters are usually made of fiberglass and are susceptible to freezing. Also, you're adding another pump to the system, which means more electricity and just another contraption to break. Of course, if you've been forced to use a pump tank in your system, you're already talking about two pumps, so why not use it to your advantage and circulate the water from your pump tank through a sand filter before it enters your collection tank?

The Cistern Filter

Like most characters that prefer to remain out of sight, the floating cistern filter is difficult to pigeonhole. We couldn't decide where to put it in this book. Is it an in-line filter like the ones we discuss in the following chapter or is it more closely related to a roof washer? (As if it matters.)

The cistern filter capitalizes on the principle that the cleanest water in any body of water can be found between ten and sixteen inches below the surface—unless, of course, the water's not that deep. The floating filter allows the pump to draw water from this cleanest depth while it filters out dirt and debris down to 60 microns. It's connected to an external jet pump via a flexible hose.

Floating Cistern Filter

Getting the Water Out of the Tank Into Your Home

Pump It Up

It's time to put on your mathematical thinking cap once more. Although a pump's function is relatively simple—to move water—a variety of factors contrive to make its job more difficult.

Atmospheric pressure, friction and head loss all exert limits on a pump's performance (see box on Nerd's Vocabulary.) To determine which size and type of pump to use, you'll need the following information about your specific system:

1. Distance from tank to pump

Water wants to be pushed, not pulled. For this reason, your pump should be located as close to the tank as possible. If one pound of pressure can push water up 2.31 feet, this means, theoretically, that atmospheric pressure (14.7 psi at sea level) could push water

Vocabulary Lesson for Water System Nerds

The next time you want to send an entire room of people at a cocktail party into a coma, start spewing some of these definitions:

PRESSURE: the measurement of force needed to push water, typically expressed in pounds. One pound of pressure will produce 2.31 feet of head. (Uh oh, what's head?)

HEAD: the measurement of height in feet to which a certain amount of pressure can push water. It doesn't matter if this height is completely vertical or slanted; it's the total vertical feet we're interest in. One foot of head requires .433 pounds of pressure per square inch. Or one pound of pressure can push water to a height of 2.31 feet in a one-inch tube.

FLOW: What you want your rainwater to do through your household pipes especially when you're in the middle of a shower. Flow is the amount of water, typically measured in gpm (gallons per minute) or gph (gallons per hour), that's moving through your pipes, disinfection units, filters, and faucets.

ATMOSPHERIC PRESSURE: Can you imagine, that at sea level, we and everything around us has 14.7 pounds of pressure pushing down on every square inch of horizontal surface area? We're not telling you this just to make you feel more overwhelmed than usual, but because atmospheric pressure plays a big part in the suction side of your water system. Never mind how the brainiacs arrived at these numbers; just remember that if you're using a centrifugal or shallow well jet pump, install the pump absolutely no higher than 25 feet above your water source. (The lifting abilities of some deep well jet pumps can exceed this 25-foot limit, but they're much more expensive.) And you only have 25 feet to work with if your system is installed at sea level. Move on up the mountain and the height is further reduced since suction lift decreases one foot for every 1,000 feet above sea level.

up a one-inch tube almost 34 feet (14.7 x 2.31= 33.957). (And please, don't ask how this works. This is a book on rainwater collection, after all, not quantum physics.) But that's only if there's no friction and if the tube were a perfect vacuum. Well, there is and it isn't. (Nature abhors a vacuum, you know.) No matter how powerful a pump is, it can only create a partial vacuum in the tube. The bottom line? You can only count on about 25 feet of lift at sea level. And, if you've studied your vocabulary properly, you'll remember that, additionally, for every 1,000-foot increase in altitude, you lose a foot of lift.

The easiest thing to do, however, is forget all these pesky numbers—which are more crucial if you're pumping water out of a well or from a lake located down a cliff from your house—and simply put the pump next to your tank if at all possible.

The difference in elevation between the pump and collection tank will effect priming. Priming a pump involves making certain that the suction line between the pump and the source of water is completely filled with water. Even the inside of the pump itself must be filled with water. (More about priming in Chapter 6.)

Pumps do not like to suck. If the water level in the tank is lower than the pump, you're going to have a priming challenge on your hands—at least initially. A handy-dandy check valve or foot valve will hold the prime in a pump once the prime is set, much like your finger on the top of a straw will hold water in that straw. Most pumps come with very specific and explicit instructions about priming. Do yourself a big favor and read those instructions.

2. Distance between and the difference in elevation of the pump and pressure tank.

When we wrote our first edition of this book, we were clueless about how critical the distance between the pump and the pressure tank is. We wrote some flippant comment about how distance would not be a consideration unless you lived on a huge ranch and wanted to pump water from the north forty to the south eighty. We thought that because a standard 3/4 horsepower, shallow well jet pump will move water a distance of about 400 feet that the pressure tank and pump could be separated up to this lengthy distance.

Wrong, wrong, wrong.

Try four feet. Separate these two co-dependent gizmos by more than four feet and you've meddled big time with their delicate cosmic harmony. But there is a way to cure this co-dependency without years of mechanical therapy. The pressure tank clings to only one aspect of the pump—the pressure switch. You can put the pump in Amarillo and the pressure tank in Beaumont (not really) as long as the pressure switch is mounted next to the pressure tank. Of course, this complicates the electrical work a bit; the power must run first to the pressure switch and then to the pump.

3. Diameter of pipe running from pump to bladder tank

Head loss is not only a problem for those facing the guillotine. In the world of plumbing, it is the friction generated between moving water and the surrounding pipe wall. The smaller the diameter of the pipe, the greater the head loss. Add turns, the disruptive bumps and grinds of valves, fittings, and connections, and your head drops even more.

Shallow Well Jet Pumps or Multi-Stage Centrifugal Pumps
Price Tag: $300-600
The Pressure or Bladder Tank
Price Tag: $450-850

While most of us are trying to eliminate stress in our lives, your household water supply is one instance where you want to be under pressure. Not only is a shower with adequate pressure less likely to lead to premature grouchiness, some home appliances—like hot-water-on-demand heaters and washing machines—won't operate without at least 20 psi. That's where the pressure tank, also known less delicately as a bladder tank, comes in.

Although the pump itself can supply that kind of pressure, you would quickly burn up the motor if the pump had to respond every time a tap was opened or a toilet was flushed in the house. The pressure tank serves a dual function: it provides storage so the pump does not have to snap to attention every time water is demanded and it maintains pressure throughout the system when the pump isn't operating. (There are new pumps on the market called on-demand pumps that don't require a separate pressure tank. We rave about one—the Grundfos MQ—a little later in this chapter.)

If you have a water well, you probably already have a pressure tank and are familiar with its operation. For you neophytes and new-home builders, the pressure tank—typically one with a capacity around 40 gallons—has an inlet at the bottom where water is pumped in from a water source, like a well or tank. As the tank fills with water, the air above it is compressed into a smaller and smaller space. Once the pressure in the tank reaches a preset level, around 30 or 40 psi, the pressure switch automatically

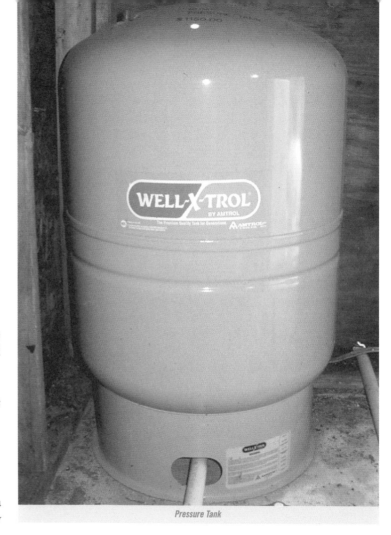

Pressure Tank

cuts off the power to the pump.

Simple galvanized tanks are still available where the air and water are in direct contact with each other. While they're cheaper than bladder tanks, they face a continual problem of becoming "waterlogged." Water in the tank will absorb air molecules, eating up the amount of air available to compress. This decreases the drawdown, which is the amount of water that is used between cycles. This causes the pump to cycle more often and wear out faster.

A bladder or diaphragm tank separates the water from the air by either encasing the water in a polypropylene bag or beneath a flexible membrane. When you get your big old strapping pressure tank, don't assume it's going to be full of water. A diaphragm tank has a maximum acceptance of .39, which means that up to 39 percent of the tank will be filled with water and the remaining 61 percent will be air.

A pressure tank can also be somewhat confusing to contemplate when hooking it up because it has a single water connection that miraculously serves as both the inlet and the outlet. A check valve near the intake keeps the water that's exiting the pressure tank from simply shooting back into your storage tank.

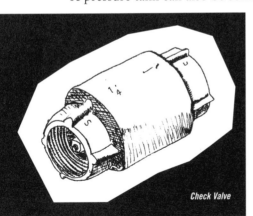

Check Valve

The New Kid on the Pumping Block: The Grundfos MQ Water Supply System
Price Tag: $500-$600

Do we have you completely confused? Well, now we're really going to mess with your head (the one on top of your neck, not the one in your collection system). Just ignore all that stuff you just tried to ingest about pressure tanks and pressure switches. Sure, in our first addition of this book, we blithely recommended a 3/4 horsepower, shallow well jet pump with a pressure switch as a nearly universal contraption for personal water systems, but now we have a new love: the Grundfos MQ water supply system. We just can't sing the praises of this little workhorse loudly enough.

This diminutive outfit combines a pump, motor, controller and pressure tank into one integral unit. Wait a minute, a pressure tank? Yep, with this pump you say bye-bye to the old pressure tank and its needy demands to be close to the pressure switch. (And you say hello to the money you didn't have to spend on a pressure tank.)

The Grundfos pump is self-priming, has a check valve incorporated in the suction port, and features a user-friendly control panel, along with over-temperature and dry-running protection. (We can't tell you how many unhappy people have run their tanks dry and burned up their shallow well jet pumps.) It's also very quiet, uses only 1000 watts of power, and can be adapted to 110 or 220 volts. And all you have to know about electricity to hook it up is how to plug an appliance into a wall outlet. Perhaps best of all, the Grundfos is expressly approved for use with rainwater, which has a tendency to attack lesser pumps.

Grundfos Pump

Chapter 5

Your Personal Clean Water Act

I F YOU AREN'T FRUSTRATED yet by the lack of hard and fast answers to rainwater collection questions, you will be now that we've entered the murky arena of filtering and disinfecting —frustrated and maybe a little scared. For every expert who demands sterilization with chlorine, a disinfectant that has been used to treat drinking water since 1908 in the United States, you'll find a conflicting report noting chlorine's inclination to react with organic matter like soil and decaying leaves in the water to create "disinfection by-products," such as chloroform and nasty trihalomethanes (THMs). These by-products may cause rectal, bladder and pancreatic cancers, as well as birth defects in humans. (They have in laboratory rats.)

For every person who proposes that no treatment is necessary because their ancestors used untreated cistern water and "if it was good enough for our grandparents, it's good enough for us," you'll find estimates linking hundreds of thousands of deaths over the years to contaminated cistern water.

Some folks swear by disinfection using ultraviolet light, some sing the praises of ozone, and others can't live without both.

It's good to know the basics. Treating water typically

Contamination is not isolated to rainwater collection systems:

- Between 1986 and 1994, the federal Centers for Disease Control and Prevention recorded 116 outbreaks of waterborne diseases in municipal and well water that sickened more than 450,000 individuals.
- In 1999, more than 1,000 people fell ill at a county fair in upstate New York after ingesting an extremely virulent strain of *E. coli* bacteria; a three-year-old girl and an elderly man died.
- Increased rainfall and a water filtration system malfunction caused a 1993 outbreak of Cryptosporidium, a microbiologic contaminant, in Milwaukee, Wisconsin. More than 400,000 illnesses and 54 deaths were linked to the contaminated drinking water.
- In the winter of 2003, residents of Athens, Ohio, regularly received warnings to boil their municipal water before drinking.
- In Walkerton, Ontario, Canada, seven people died and 2,300 became ill in May 2000 after excessive rainfall caused runoff to contaminate a well, resulting in an outbreak of *E. coli* O157: H7.

involves two processes: disinfection, which kills all living things in the water, like those sickening bacteria and viruses; and conditioning, which removes inert particles, minerals, and chemicals. Effective treatment of rainwater usually involves both of these processes.

All Filters Are Not Created Equal
Price Tag: $30-50 for cartridge filter with housing

Some filters are as simple as they sound, merely screening out sediment like dirt, sand, and rust. Once enough of these chunks

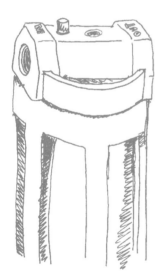

have accumulated, the filter material is tossed out. Curiously enough, these basic filters are called "pre-filters". Perhaps this is a hint that they alone will not do the entire job of treating your water. The most common types of pre-filters for rainwater treatment are cartridge filters. Often they are strung along in-line, beginning with a big bruiser, like a pool filter made of pleated plastic, which will remove all particles in the 50-100 micron range. One or more cartridge filters follow with smaller and smaller pores; typically the final filter

Close-up Filter Housing

will remove all particles up to 3 microns in size.

Cootie Patrol
The next most common line of defense in the rainwater treatment scenario is the activated carbon filter, which is made from a variety of carbon-based materials, the most obvious being coal and the most intriguing being fruit pits and coconut husks. These materials are steamed to high temperatures without the use of oxygen, a process that creates a surface full of microscopic holes and nooks and crannies. The pores trap large molecules and microscopic particles, while smaller organic molecules are absorbed by the activated surface. In theory, activated charcoal can absorb odors and tastes, and if the pores are small enough, even remove protozoa or cysts (yuk) that might find their way into your rainwater.

For this theory to work in real life, the filters must be

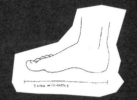

How big is one micron?

It's one-millionth of a meter or three-millionths of a foot...

or one-fifth the size of an average American bacteria.

or one one-hundredth the diameter of a human hair...

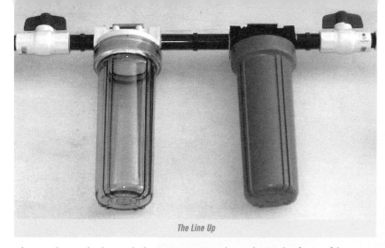
The Line Up

changed regularly and the water must be relatively free of heavy organic sediments (i.e. pre-filtered) before it gets to the charcoal filter. Otherwise, the filter can actually become a breeding ground and feeding station for low-life bacteria. In fact, some sources recommend sterilization by chlorination or UV light before the water is allowed to pass through the activated charcoal filter. (We don't.)

Silver is added to some activated charcoal filters in an attempt to thwart bacterial growth. Pioneers traveling across the United States believed so strongly in the antiseptic ability of silver they would drop silver dollars in the barrels of water they carried in their wagons in an attempt to keep their water supply from going bad. But because silver is toxic to humans as well as bacteria, the amount of the heavy metal that can be added to the filter is minimal and any claims by manufacturers that it will "absolutely and in all cases inhibit bacterial growth" should be viewed with a healthy dose of skepticism. According to a

report by the Federal Trade Commission, studies on the effectiveness of bacteriostatic (silver) filters "have shown unpromising results as to their ability to control bacterial growth."

Remember, fear and greed are two of the greatest motivators, an object lesson not lost on a breed of filter salesmen who avariciously play on people's fears of contaminated water. The result? Deceitful tactics used to sell water filters abound. Choose your filters carefully and never ever buy a water treatment system from a telemarketer. And never ever let a salesman in your home to do a "free" water test. According to an article in *Garbage Magazine* (March/April 1991), this test is "like a hocus-pocus magic show: It's meant to mystify you, but it won't tell you whether life threatening contaminants have infiltrated your water." The magic show usually involves filling a test tube with your water and adding a chemical that will either react with chlorine or harmless minerals with dazzling results: your water turns yellow or precipitates solids. Then the magician sells you a $75-filter of little merit for $493.

Filters and Flow

Typically, the water pressure in your supply line is around 30 to 50 psi. This amount of pressure should supply a household with enough water to meet peak demand. Then you go and add a filter. As you can imagine, a filter cartridge that can remove particles as small as 3 microns is going to place some restriction on your flow. Why are we worrying you with this now? So you can size your filters and filter housings accordingly.

In the strange world of filters, where one filter restricts your flow, the addition of more filters will increase your flow rate.

This trick doesn't work, however, by stringing more filters in line, but by stacking filters within a single chamber. We get along fine with the restrictions placed on our flow by two ten-inch long filters: first, a 5-micron sediment filter, followed by a 3-micron activated charcoal filter. Then again, there's just the two of us. A larger family with greater peak demands may not. Without increasing the water pressure, you can increase your flow by installing filter housings that are twice as long (typically 20 inches) and filling each with two cartridges. How does this work? By allowing the water to flow through twice the area of filter media, kind of like the difference between a crowd leaving a concert hall through five exits as opposed to ten.

There are a few things to remember if you decided to bump up your flow this way. For one thing, it will cost twice as much every time you change your filters (and they have to be changed just as often). Also, if you are using an ultraviolet light for disinfection (discussed below) you want to make certain that you don't exceed the recommended flow for your UV unit.

Ultraviolet Light
Price Tag: $400-$1000

And here you thought we should be avoiding UV light. Now someone suggests you buy a machine that generates it! But there's a beneficial side to this skin-wrinkling spectrum in the world of water treatment. And it's not a new technology; UV has been used widely in Europe for drinking water disinfection since the early 1900s. When water is circulated in front of an ultraviolet lamp, bacteria and viruses are killed instantly.

Ultraviolet Light

Recent studies now credit ultraviolet light as an effective treatment for cysts such as Cryptosporidium and Giardia, not by killing the organisms outright, but by cracking their protective shells and rendering them unable to reproduce. Bruce Macler, of the EPA, was quoted by the American Water Works Association as touting UV technology "because it's cheap, reliable, benign, leaves no DBPs, and is effective against Cryptosporidium." James Malley, a researcher with the University of New Hampshire concurs: "We have reams of data on UV's effects on crypto. All with the same basic message: 'Yeah, it works.'"

But UV is only effective if the light hits its targets and several factors can shield the bacteria from the deadly light. Tiny particles of sediment, some no larger than 5 microns, can run interference for microorganisms who hide in their shadows. For this reason, water must be filtered before it enters the UV disinfecting chamber. If the bacterial count is higher than 1,000 coliforms per 100 milliliter, some bacteria will be shielded by other sacrificial or kamikaze bacteria.

Also, the quartz sleeve or glass surrounding and protecting the UV lamp must be cleaned regularly. Some well-engineered UV lights are designed with wiper units so that the sleeve can be wiped clean, simply by sliding it in and out of the unit three times, without having to disassemble the unit.

UV disinfection comes highly recommended by many in the rainwater collection business because it treats water without the use of chemicals, without introducing any unpleasant taste or odor, and because it consumes minimal power. And you won't choke on the purchase price.

UV lamps are rated by the gallons per minute they can disinfect. For residential units, this ranges from 4 gpm up to 36 gpm. When shopping for your personal source of sunlight, look for a unit that disinfects at least 12 gallons per minute. This is usually more than adequate if you have a 3-micron activated charcoal filter in-line prior to the UV light. If you plan on stacking filters—as we discussed earlier—to increase your flow, you need to increase the capacity of your UV unit accordingly. You can also purchase gizmos that are installed in-line that will restrict the flow to meet your exact demands.

Some UV lights come with alarms to let you know when the water isn't being zapped properly due to the diminished effectiveness of your bulb. (Like us, these bulbs dim over time.) The alarm monitors the intensity of the bulb and sounds a warning when it has fallen below an acceptable level. These alarms can be expensive, however. If you want to cut costs, just be sure to change your bulb after at least every 10,000 hours of operation or after 14 months of use. And don't rely on a visual inspection of the bulb to determine whether to change it or not.

People tell us all the time that they didn't change their bulb for several years because it "still looked bright enough." Hey, unless you're a bacteria, you won't be able to detect the effectiveness—or lack thereof—of a UV bulb. Just change it.

Ozone
Price Tag: $700 to $2600

Ozone is a form of oxygen having three atoms per molecule rather than the two in atmospheric oxygen. According to one report, ozone is a more powerful germicide than chlorine, reduces iron, manganese, lead and sulfur in water, and eliminates foul tastes and odors. According to most studies, its effectiveness is not affected by pH or temperature. Sound too good to be true?

Point of Use Ultraviolet Light

We have not been impressed with the few point-of-use ultraviolet lights we've seen. For one thing, they're comparatively expensive; for a few bucks more you can buy a UV unit that will disinfect the water supplied to your entire house instead of just the drinking water at the kitchen sink. (Not to mention the little problem of brushing your teeth in the un-disinfected bathroom or opening your mouth in the un-disinfected shower.) Also, the disinfecting lamp is inserted in the equivalent of a small filter housing. This lamp gets hot and it naturally heats up the water. How about a nice tepid glass of water in the middle of August? We've also heard that replacement parts can be very hard to find and that few (if any) come with an intensity meter to monitor the disinfecting power of the lamp. (Remember: Just because the lamp is glowing, that doesn't necessarily mean it's working properly. The bulbs are only effective for about 14 months or 10,000 hours.)

Well, not if you read another report that says that excessive amounts of iron, manganese, and sulfur (seldom a problem in rainwater systems) interfere with the disinfection process. Also, high turbidity in the water limits ozone's effectiveness. This creates problems if you're trying to treat an entire collection tank of rainwater that hasn't been pre-filtered. Plus, ozone has such a brief shelf life as a disinfectant that sufficient contact time with the water can be difficult to obtain. The O-3 molecule doesn't like to just hang around; it's a gas, always seeking the atmosphere. In 15 minutes or less, the restless O-3 molecule has traveled through the water and out of the tank into the big, wide world. So the ozone must be mixed immediately throughout the water using an elaborate system that includes not only the generator, but also diffuser stones or rings and a pump. (Ah, another pump. That means more complications and more electricity, right? Is that a good thing?)

Another bone we have to pick with ozone is that it is very difficult to monitor its effectiveness without either frequently testing water samples using reagents or installing an expensive in-line monitor ($1200 or more).

The Voice of Experience

On a personal note, we have an ozone "generating" unit (not to be confused with an ozone "generator") that we use to help disinfect our hot tub. It does a decent job, but we still have to use bromine tablets. The unit would probably work much better if, instead of the water passing by the generating lamp on its way to the tub, the ozone was injected directly into the tub using a diffuser stone. This would give the O-3 molecules more time to

Sunbathing Cooties

work their magic on a tub full of bugs. Units like this, which operate within water storage tanks, are available, but they're expensive—as much as $5000 and up.

Of the 33 case studies sited in the *Texas Guide to Rainwater Harvesting*, only one uses ozone treatment for disinfection. The majority of those systems that use any treatment at all rely on a combination of filters and ultraviolet light. Dr. Hari Krishna, a senior engineer at the Texas Water Development Board, was quoted in an article by the Lower Colorado River Authority as follows: "In general we recommend that for indoor use, a homeowner install a cartridge filter to remove sediment and a

Clorox Bottle

carbon filter to reduce odors, followed by a UV (ultraviolet) light for disinfection."

Chlorination

Price Tag: $1/month manual dose to $3,000 for a complete automatic self-dosing system

We sat next to a ninety-six-year-old woman on an airplane recently. We were talking about how much the world had changed over her long lifetime. When we asked her what she thought was the best invention or product created in this century, she said, without a moment's hesitation, "Clorox!" People in the water treatment business aren't nearly so universally enthusiastic in their endorsement of chlorine.

In the book *Planning for an Individual Water System*, the author writes that one reason why "health authorities in general favor chlorine disinfection over other disinfection methods" is because "the chlorine residual lasts for a long period of time after leaving the disinfection unit thus providing continuing protection."

It's this very "continuing protection" that worries other authorities on the subject. Stu Campbell also touts chlorine's superior disinfecting qualities in *The Home Water Supply*: "Those with any knowledge of water will agree that disinfection, where needed, is the most important water-treatment process, and that chlorination is by far the most popular method of disinfection."

Although Campbell asserts that "there seems to be no vastly superior alternative to chlorination," he at least acknowledges chlorine's dark side. "When combined with organic matter it forms substances called trihalomethanes, which, sure enough, cause cancer in laboratory mice. More recently, an EPA study released in December 1980, links heavy chlorination to bladder, colon, and intestinal cancer."

And Scott Alan Lewis, author of *The Sierra Club Guide to Safe Drinking Water*, writes of 10,000 cases of rectal and bladder cancers that may have been caused by chlorine disinfection by-products.

In *Cottage Water Systems*, Max Burns calls chlorine a "chemical streetwalker—always looking for a mate, and you know it's going to cost." He's not only concerned with our direct contact with the nasty offspring of these unions (THMs) in drinking water; he's worried about the formation of the buggers throughout the environment: "Because the water we treat inevitably ends up in our septic system [or storm drains or rivers or aquifers], which is essentially an ocean of organic compounds, the likelihood of forming these potentially carcinogenic compounds is high, as is the likelihood of some of these newly created toxins leaching out into the environment." And even if you escape chlorine-related toxins on a personal level, the manufacturing of chlorine creates dioxins that have to go somewhere.

Although it takes relatively small amounts of chlorine, measured in parts per million, to disinfect rainwater, there are a couple of things to consider when dosing: the turbidity of or Total Dissolved Solids (TDS) in the water and the amount of time chlorine must be in contact with the water. Filtering the water before (and after?) chlorination easily solves the turbidity problem.

The time constraints are trickier to address. There are two types of chlorination procedures: simple chlorination and superchlorination. For simple chlorination, small doses of chlorine, around .5 to 1 PPM, are added to water so that .2 to .5 parts per million residual chlorine remain. It's this leftover chlorine which kills bacteria and viruses (and combines with organic matter to form THMs). For doses within this concentration, the chlorine must remain in contact with the water for at least 20 to 30 minutes.

We could go on and on about chlorine, but honestly, what's the point? With all the other options at your disposal, we think you'd be nuts to disinfect your rainwater with chlorine. So we're going to do you a favor and stop this discussion right here.

Reverse Osmosis
Price Tag: $400-1500

We have a reverse osmosis (RO) system connected to our kitchen faucet and the icemaker in our freezer. Many folks in the rainwater collection business have told us that this is plain stupid, that rainwater, properly filtered and disinfected by one or more of the aforementioned processes, is too pure to require RO. We have read several books and articles that claim that RO will waste 50-75 percent of the tap water put into them: "For one gallon of RO filtered water, it may take four gallons or more of tap water." (We now know that the higher the quality of the RO, the less water will be lost in the discharge stream.) We have read that the filters will clog quickly and are expensive to maintain. All that said, let us tell you what it's really like outside the pedantic world of textbooks and expert opinion. (Although we're not great fans of anecdotal evidence, sometimes it's worth listening to.)

When we had our RO system filtering the heavily-chlorinated

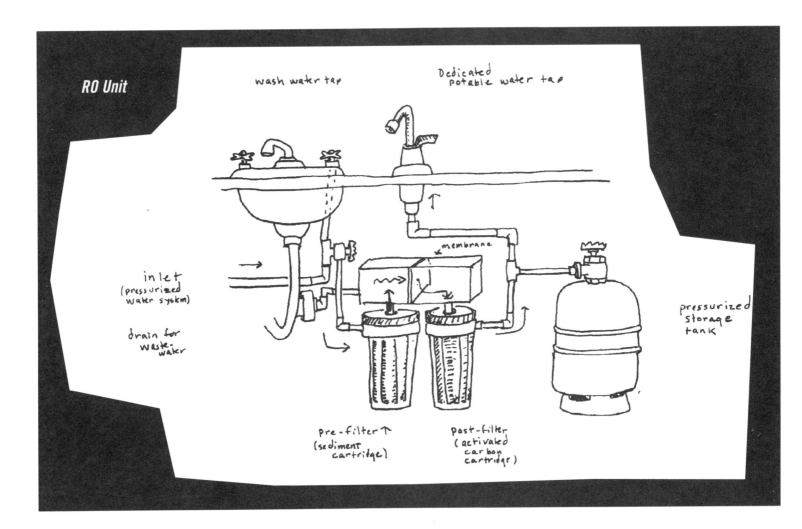

wash water tap

Dedicated
potable water tap

inlet
(pressurized
water system)

drain for
waste-
water

membrane

pre-filter ↑
(sediment
cartridge)

post-filter
(activated
carbon
cartridge)

pressurized
storage
tank

municipal water at our former residence, we did "waste" at least four times the water as we treated. The filters did need to be changed more often than the manufacturer suggested.

Then we moved to our present location and ran our well water through the RO unit. The poor thing gurgled all day trying to spit out a cup of clean water and the membrane was clogged in about three days. (No lie.)

Then we hooked up to our rainwater system and the RO unit hit its stride. We haven't changed the membrane in, oh, six years. (Don't tell anyone.) We discharge about a quarter cup of water for every two gallons of treated water we use. Well, you say, maybe they're right to tell you it's not necessary. Maybe it works so efficiently because the water is already perfect.

Maybe.

But why then, in very unscientific, but blind taste tests, is the RO water more refreshing and sweeter than the water out of the bathroom tap? Why will we cross an outdoor breezeway from our bedroom to the kitchen in the middle of the night in the dead of winter to refill our water glass from the RO faucet rather than from the one in the bathroom?

Well, it might be because of the wacky way we built our house, tucked into those debris-dropping trees, with more downspouts and bends and turns than we can keep clean. We think, because of our particularly humus-happy environment, that even after filtration through a 5-micron sediment filter and a 3-micron activated charcoal filter, our water contains just enough dissolved solids to make it taste only good, not perfect. The RO unit pushes it to perfection, removing particles down to .001 of a micron. That's smaller than any virus, bacteria, pollen, lint ball, or any other thing your body would prefer not to ingest.

We also wonder if, because of rainwater's inherent slightly corrosive nature, that we're tasting traces of our plumbing pipes when we drink from the bathroom sink.

Still not convinced that we should use R.O.? Then come on over and taste for yourself.

Chapter 6

The Set Up

Chapter 6 The Set Up

YOU'VE CHOSEN YOUR SITE, your pumps and your treatment system. Now it's time to hook the whole mess together. For this job, you'll be wearing your plumber, electrician, ditch digger and errand boy (or girl) hats.

I've Got One Word for You: Plastic

Throughout the years, our pipe of choice has been PVC (polyvinyl chloride) and CPVC (for hot water lines). It is easy

for the do-it-yourselfer to cut and connect, is readily available and reasonably priced, has little internal friction, and resists breaking during a hard freeze better than galvanized or copper pipe. It also resists the corrosive nature of rainwater. (Because it is slightly acidic and extremely soft, rainwater has the tendency to attack metal pipes. More on rainwater's dark side in Chapter 7.)

And yes, we know PVC isn't perfect, that its manufacturing process is the poster child for environmental evil. Some folks

even believe that it contaminates water that runs through it, although no research has shown this to be the case. But what, exactly, were the alternatives?

Until recently, nothing practically speaking. But a couple of new options are on the horizon—if not closer. One is a composite water piping that has recently become more available in the United States after, of course, many years of happy use overseas. (For a country packed with technological geniuses, we are sometimes so slow to catch on to new products.) Made from an aluminum tube that is laminated to interior and exterior layers of polyethylene plastic, the piping is lightweight, can operate at pressures up to 300 psi, and can be used for hot and cold water. You can run it indoors in the slab, walls, and attic, and outdoors as long as it is protected from UV light. (That means you have to bury it.) It's easily bent or formed by hand and is available in diameters between ⅜ and one inch. Because it's flexible and comes in 100-foot rolls, fewer fittings are needed, which equals fewer potential leaks and less friction loss. Manufacturers also claim that composite piping can reduce hot water delivery time by up to 18 percent when compared to copper piping.

The other type of pipe that's showing up more and more is PEX or cross-linked polyethylene pipe. (This is not to be confused with cross-linked polybutylene pipe that was used to disastrous effect in radiant-floor systems in the seventies; it ruptured under exposure to chlorine. Can you say "jackhammer the slab"?) PEX has undergone over 30 years of testing and has yet to fail under normal conditions. It boasts the same advantages—easy to install, fewer fittings than copper or PVC, etc—as the composite pipe. Like composite piping, it too is immune to corrosion.

Now for the downside of these newbies. Besides the fact that we don't know if the manufacturing process is any more environmentally friendly than that of PVC, the cost of the composite and PEX piping is higher than PVC, more along the same price as copper. The materials still aren't as readily available to home handypersons, it requires specialized tools to install, and some building official may be unfamiliar with it. But considering all that these two products have going for them, surely it's only a matter of time before they gain universal acceptance.

Until that time, we're stuck with PVC.

We recommend the rigid variety of PVC. A flexible type, often used to plumb whirlpool spas and such, is also available. We once thought this stuff was the greatest thing for quickly connecting rainwater components together that can sometimes wind up positioned at odd angles to each other. After repairing about a zillion leaks in pressurized lines, we are no longer in awe of this flexible type—although it's still okay to use it in unpressurized situations, like for suction lines or when connecting tanks together.

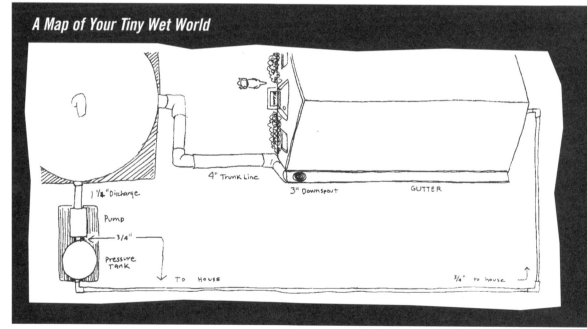

A Map of Your Tiny Wet World

4" Trunk Line

3" Downspout

GUTTER

1 1/2" Discharge

Pump

3/4"

Pressure Tank

TO HOUSE

3/4" to house

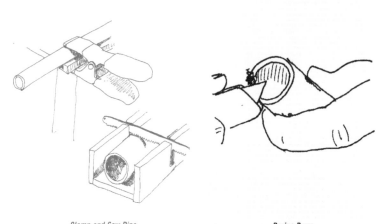

Clamp and Saw Pipe *Paring Burrs*

Glue Pipe

pipe. (Some how-to books suggest you bevel the outside of the end "so it will not force the glue from the inside of the fitting," but we think these are the same people who check the air in their car tires every day.) You may want to invest in a pair of PVC cutters which cut clean without any burr problem. If the pipe or fitting is especially dirty, wipe it clean and check for fit.

Otherwise, don't use it and don't ever mention it to us again. It's too painful to admit we were wrong.

You may be tempted to sketch out your plumbing schematic in precise detail in an attempt to buy all the needed parts on one trip to the hardware store. This can certainly cut back on your treks, but you'll be less frustrated if you realize you'll be beating a path to the plumbing department over and over again for one more 90-degree slip elbow or ¾-inch coupling until you finish the project.

You'll want to pick a day when the temperature is above 40 degrees to start gluing the pipes together since cold slows the action of PVC solvent-cement. Also, if it's too cold you'll be shivering and you won't be able to make precision cuts on the pipe.

Although PVC fittings allow some leeway for wobbly saw cuts, try to be as accurate as possible when slicing through the pipe. After cutting, pare away any burrs from the inside of the

When you have the fittings and pipe line up how you like them, you can make positioning marks on them with an indelible marker so you can quickly slap them back into exactly the same position once you've slathered the end of the pipe and inside the fitting with, first, primer, and then a thick—but not too thick—coat of cement. Be gentle when you slather the cement and primer over the mark you've made or you'll erase it. Also, you'll want to avoid letting the glue build up or puddle. Not only is it a waste of glue, but excess glue may leech trace amounts of tetrahydrofuron into your rainwater when you first fire up your system. This chemical is so noxious you might be able to smell it even after the tainted water has passed through an activated carbon filter.

PVC Anatomy 101

DON'T WORRY: nothing gory about this anatomy. Just nice clean white plastic elbows and such. The only thing that might confuse you about the fittings is that they come in two varieties: pressure fittings which don't have flanges on the ends and fittings for pipe that's not under pressure, like the trunkline, which do have flanges on the ends.

elbow

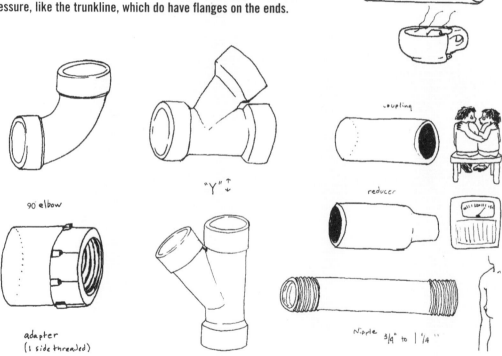

90 elbow

"Y"

adapter
(1 side threaded)

coupling

reducer

Nipple 3/4" to 1 1/4"

HINT: There are no awards handed out for jamming fittings together. Leave a little length of plain old pipe—about three inches long—between the fittings so you can more easily make corrections or repair future leaks.

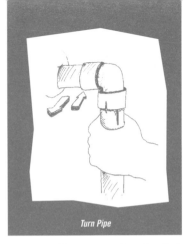

Turn Pipe

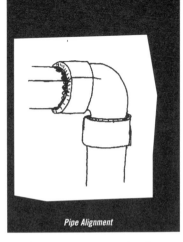

Pipe Alignment

You'll want to give the fitting or pipe a quarter turn back-and-forth to help spread the glue around. One clue that you've done everything right to make your joint leak free is the "bead" of glue that appears at the edge of the fitting. The more complete and uniform the bead is all the way around, the better the glue job.

Organizing All Your Stuff

There are two ways to set up your system: 1) put all the stuff down by the collection tanks in a little pump house or 2) put all the stuff in the garage or a room of the house designated as the pump/filter room. (For some reason, we call this the mechanical room.)

Of course, there are variations on these two themes. At our house, for instance, the pump is located by the tanks in a shelter that looks like a glorified dog house and the pressure tank, filters, and such are located in a mechanical room we designed into our house for just this purpose. Several contingencies will guide you in your location decision. Are you currently on a well? If you

are, you probably already have a pump house where your bladder tank, tons of water softening equipment, and your old tennis rackets and broken tricycles are stored. It makes sense to convert this space into your rainwater nerve center since it can be heated during freezing weather, the equipment is protected, and the water line to your house originates here.

Maybe you've designed a new house with rainwater collection in mind, but you located the mechanical room next to the office/guest room (like we did) and the sound of the pump would drive an office worker or overnight visitor crazy, so you decide to split the components up (like we did.)

Or perhaps your tanks are far from your house, farther than a reasonably-priced pump could pull the water, so you're forced by physics to hook the pump up close to the tanks. (Remember: Pumps like to push water. By placing your pump as close to the water source as possible, you take advantage of that 14.7 psi of atmospheric pressure and reduce suction head-loss. Water arriving at the pump is at optimum pressure, resulting in less wear and tear on the pump.)

If you decide to put the whole system out by the tanks, it's a good idea to build a little pallet—concrete or treated wood will do. You can bolt your pump down to this pallet. And bolt it down good; the manufacturers didn't put all those bolt holes in the footing of the pump for the fun of it. Nothing tears up a masterpiece of plumbing work faster than a pump jumping around every time it turns on.

But don't bolt it down yet. First, run pipe out of the outlet hole on your tank. The fittings you need for this will vary depending on the type of collection tank you have. There is typically a 1 ½-inch

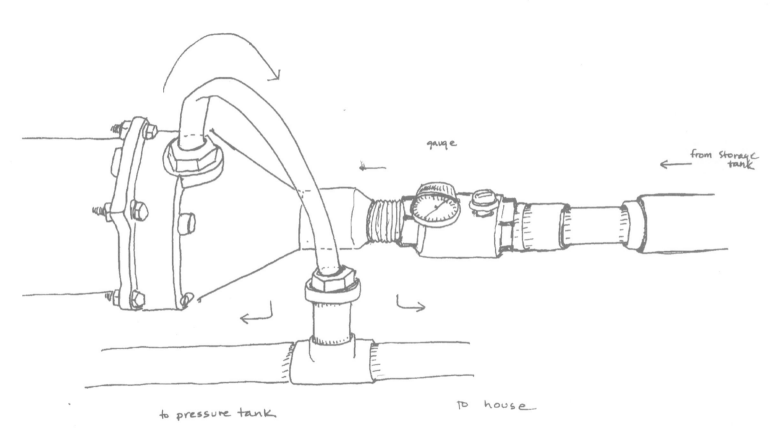

gauge

from storage tank

to pressure tank

to house

female fitting on the bottom of the fiberglass tanks we sell. Screw a male adapter into this hole, then reduce the line to fit your pump's suction requirements. Large jet pumps require a 1 ¼-inch or sometimes even a 1 ½-inch inlet. And always remember: if your pump is a serious distance away from your tank, you will have to size the suction pipe to compensate for any friction loss.

Check Valve at Tank

Next, stick on a ball valve near the outlet of the tank so you can shut off the flow from your tank anytime you need to, like when that riffraff brother-in-law trips on a length of your plumbing pipe and breaks it. Be sure to use a ball valve to reduce friction loss; an "economy" globe valve can create as much friction as a 50-foot length of pipe.

If the pump is more than a couple of feet from the collection

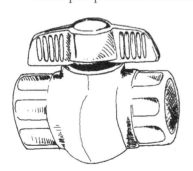

Behold the Simple Beauty of the Ball Valve

tank, a check valve will need to be installed at the outlet of the tank. This will simplify priming the pump because you can then manually fill the line from the pump to the tank with water, with the check valve locking the water in the suction line where you need it.

If your pump is up close and personal to your tank, just run a little length of pipe and put in a check valve right at the pump. (Make sure it runs the right way! The arrow on the check valve should point away from the tank and towards the pump. You wouldn't believe how often this simple rule is ignored, leading to complete frustration and tearing of hair when trying to start up the system.) Then, face the pump towards the tank and hook it up. The largest hole is almost always the suction port. Use the fewest possible fittings—especially elbows—when connecting the pipe from the water supply (the tank) to the suction port.

Come out of the pump discharge hole with a flexible stainless steel supply line. Not only does this stainless line simplify the plumbing connections, but its flexibility comes in handy in a variety of circumstances, such as when you're priming the

Check Valve at Pump

Too Much Pressure

Those boys at the pressure tank company are sometimes a little heavy-handed when it comes to pre-charging your pressure tank. It's up to you to counteract their exuberance. The tank needs to be charged to two pounds less than the "cut in" pressure of your pump. Most pumps turn on at 30 psi, so most pressure tanks need to be filled with 28 psi. Too much or too little pressure and the pump will cycle on and off erratically. To check the pressure in the tank, first drain out all the water, then press a handy tire gauge onto the valve at the top of the tank. Pffffff. Let out enough air to bring your reading down to 28 psi (or whatever is 2 psi below your pump's cut-in pressure). If you let out too much air, you can increase the pressure in the tank with a handy bicycle pump.

pump and need to fill the pump head with water. It also makes for a quick and easy disconnect if (when, really) you need to repair or replace your pump.

From this stainless line, you'll next be heading to the pressure tank and filter housings. (Note: If you're using the nifty Grundfos pump, it comes with its own built-in pressure tank).

To connect the pressure tank, install a "tee" in the line running to your filters. Now, we're aware that this doesn't sound quite right, to simply "tee" off to the pressure tank. It seems like the water should run through the pressure tank, right? In one hole and out another. But remember the pressure tank only has one water connection that serves as both the inlet and outlet. Since the water doesn't go "through" the tank, it can be attached via a tee anywhere along the supply line between the pump and the filters, preferably as close to

Pump With Flexible Stainless Steel Supply Line

the pump as possible.

When it comes to installing your filter housings, don't even think about supporting them with plumbing lines alone. This set-up will prove much less than ideal when it comes time to unscrew the filtering housings to change the cartridges. Sometimes these housings have the magical ability to over-tighten themselves. (No human will ever admit to being so heavy-handed.) Sometimes the torque needed to unscrew the housing is enough to snap your plumbing lines right off if they're supported by nothing but themselves and air, not known for its structural integrity.

So, if you're installing your equipment out by the tank and pump, go ahead and build a wall to attach your filter housings to. (After all, they do come with such nice brackets for this very purpose.)

And you might as well consider your wall part of a little house you'll need to build to protect your pump, pipes, and precious parts from freezing. Make it big enough to accommodate you, all your stuff, and the elbow room you'll need to change out the filter cartridges in their housings, tinker with the pump, and generally bang on things when they don't seem to be working right. And whatever you do, be sure to allow enough room in the house so that you can change out the bulb in your UV light, which typically must slide all the way out of one side of the unit. But make the house small enough so that it can be heated with a couple of 100-watt light bulbs during those occasional, short-lived very hard freezes we have here. (If you live in the land of really arctic weather, we're sure you realize your freeze protection must go much further than this.)

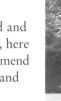

Neighbor's Dog with Little Pumphouse

Before you rush ahead and attach your filter housings, here are a few gadgets we recommend you install in-line before (and after) the filter housings:

Pump Hiding Under Fake Rock

You'll want to stick a ball valve in before the first filter housing and after the second filter housing. (Honestly, we don't have stock in the Ball Valve Company.) We've learned through hard-won experience that you can't have enough opportunities to isolate different components of your water system. And can you imaging trying to change your filters without shutting off the water to them?

You may also want to include a pressure gauge before and after the filter housings. These gauges come in handy if you want to monitor the flow restriction caused by your filters (the dirtier the filter gets, the greater the difference in pressure readings between the two gauges). They can also help you detect any leaks that might occur in your pressure lines on either side of the gauges. (See Chapter 7.)

If your pump is some distance from the rest of your equipment, you might even want to stick a third pressure gauge directly on the pump. (And no, we also don't own stock in Acme Pressure Gauge, Inc.)

Another nifty thing you might want to include somewhere in-line between the pump and the filters is a "tee" for a hose bib. This will come in handy when you want to use unfiltered water to wash the car or water the house plants.

We figure we've probably hooked up about a zillion of these filter housings. Want to know how we do it? First, prior to hanging the filter housings, we connect them using a 6-inch long ¼-inch schedule 90 nipple (it's the gray stuff; never have seen it in white). Most standard filter housings have a ¾-inch inlet and outlet, but check the ones you're using to be sure. And make sure you're connecting the outlet of the clear sediment filter housing (the first in line) to the inlet of the opaque filter housing (the second in line and the one that holds the activated carbon filter). The outlet will either have the word "out" or an arrow pointing away from the center of the filter housing and the inlet will either have the word "in" or an arrow pointing towards the center of the filter housing. Clear as mud? Good, let's continue.

Now, screw a 3-inch long ¾-inch schedule 80 nipple into the inlet of the clear housing. Screw a ¾-inch threaded ball valve to this. Repeat these steps on the outlet of the opaque housing (the only hole left). Then, screw a ¾-inch close nipple (a little short one) into the end of each of the ball valves. At this point, we rely on a kind of weird fitting: a ¾-inch 90-degree elbow that has a female thread on one end (which attaches to the close nipple) and a glue fitting on the other end (to which we can attach ¾-inch PVC pipe).

All the components

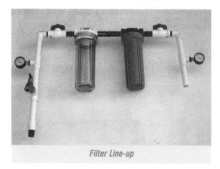

Filter Line-up

From the 90-degree fitting closest to the opaque filter, you'll be heading either directly to your house's plumbing supply lines or—we hope—to one or more of the water treatment gizmos we described in Chapter 5: a UV light, an ozone generator, or—yuck—a chlorine doser. (The reverse osmosis unit is a point-of-use treatment only, to be attached under your kitchen sink.)

If you must know—and you must since we're pretending to be experienced experts here and we're writing the book—we strongly prefer the UV light for disinfection. But if you insist on using chlorine treatment, you'll probably also want a second activated charcoal filter between it and the ultimate destination—your mouth. When installing a UV light, there's something very important you must remember: the lamp in the unit will have to be changed periodically. You must leave enough room to slide the lamp—typically nearly the same length as the unit—all the way out of the unit. Glass bulbs do not bend no matter how you hold your tongue during the procedure. Also, don't try to plumb everything up as tightly as possible—like snugging fittings right next to each other with the shortest length of pipe possible. Leave yourself a little wiggle room—at least a couple of inches—so that you can cut out mistakes (Heaven's forbid!) or repair immediate or future leaks.

Also try to remember one more thing when you're in the midst of this plumbing nightmare. (We're just kidding. Really, plumbing is fun.) The supply line, which is the water line to the house after pressurization, is usually ¾-inch or greater in diameter depending on how far you have to run the line. Friction—which, remember, is influenced by pipe length, flow rate, and fittings—tries to stop the water from going by. So the longer the run, the bigger the pipe has to be. Oddly enough, it makes no difference that once the water line gets to the house it is typically reduced down to 3/4 or one inch. What you're trying to do is get a greater volume of water coming in than you can possibly use even if two people are taking a shower and you are doing a load of laundry and there is a kid out washing the dog.

If you have a well, your supply line to the house is already there for you. Unless your well is completely inoperable, you probably don't want to disconnect it entirely. Instead, cut the supply line and glue in a "tee". One side will go back to the discharge from your well and the other will go to the outlet port on your new "rainwater pump." But there's one thing you must do: put a ball valve between each source and the "tee." This way when it comes time to put the power to your new pump, you should be able to use the same electrical circuit for both the well pump and rainwater pump. Simply turning off one valve or the other will control the source of your water.

Caveat: If you space out and leave both valves open, you'll mix your precious, pristine rainwater with your stinky well water. And it's so hard to sort out those water molecules when this happens.

Cup of Molecules

How Much Water Is in the Tank?

If you aren't obsessive-compulsive yet, you will be when it comes to checking on your water supply. Rather than thump on the side of the tank like you're picking out a melon or climbing up on a ladder and peering through the manhole, here's a nifty gizmo—which we've bestowed with the catchy name of "water level indicator tube"—that'll make it easy to check your supply

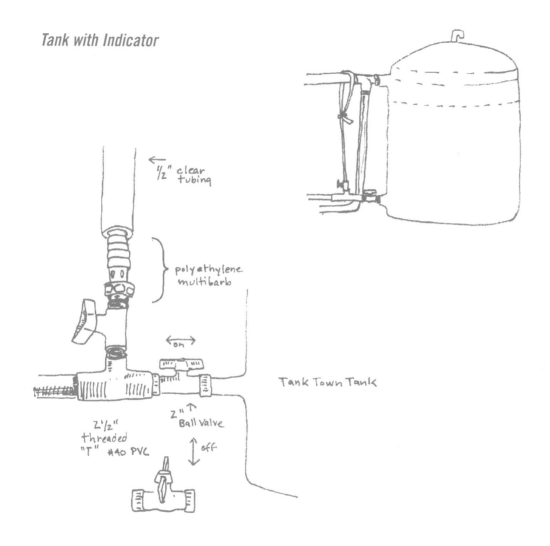

½" clear tubing

polyethylene multibarb

on

Tank Town Tank

2½" threaded "T" #40 PVC

2" Ball Valve

off

every thirty minutes without arousing the suspicions of your psychiatrist neighbor. We used to clamp the tubing in place, but now we recommend that you push the clear tubing onto the barbed fitting every time you check the water level. Once you happily discover that your tank has plenty of water, simply turn the valve off (very, very important unless you want to drain the tank) then pull the tubing off the fitting. By keeping the tubing drained, you eliminate the chance for algae to grow in it.

(Fun Note: If the humidity is just right, you can see the water level on the outside of the tank because of the *seat line* created by the difference in air and water temperature.)

Power Play

Everybody is scared of electricity. Look what it can do to the hairdo of a cartoon character, for instance, if he sticks his fork in a power outlet. But we don't think you should fear it. Respect it, but don't fear it.

There isn't much electrical work involved with a rainwater system so we're going to keep instructions here to a bare minimum. If you're using the wonderful Grundfos MQ pump, you can skip this entire section. With the Grundfos MQ, all you have to do is plug the little beauty in (you can manage that without directions, right?), fill it with water to prime, and then push the right buttons on the control panel to fire it up.

If you know absolutely nothing about electrical wiring, like even how to cut it, or you can't tell the difference between tin snips and needle nose pliers, our lawyers have asked us to tell you to hire a professional for this job or at least go to the library and check out one of the excellent books by Time Warner or Ortho on do-it-yourself basic wiring. (The owner's manuals that come with many pumps also offer great instruction for the novice as long as they're not one of those strange translations from

Taiwanese or Korean.) We're at the end of this book and we're tired, so we're going to assume at least a smidgen of prior knowledge on your part. Okay?

If you have a well and your rainwater pump is near or in the well house, you won't have to wear your electrician's hat for long since you already have power at your fingertips. Shocking, no?

If you're installing a system in a new house, you may either have power in the designated mechanical room or you may have to run underground cable (Type UF) from your main breaker box to the tank/pump outpost. You can conveniently bury this cable in the trench you've dug for your supply line. Check with a knowledgeable source— like the aforementioned how-to books—to learn how to run a new line from your breaker box.

If you're working in an existing pump house or with an existing well, your power may be running to a disconnect or circuit breaker in the pump house. But more than

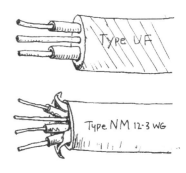

NM Type Wire

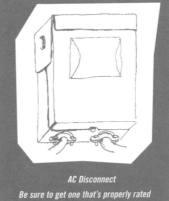

AC Disconnect
Be sure to get one that's properly rated and properly fused.

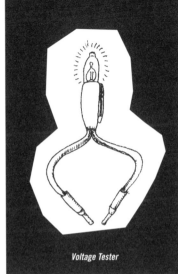

Hook Wires on Screws Clockwise

Voltage Tester

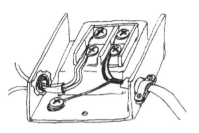

The Guts of a Pressure Switch

Next, cut a length of NM cable (2-wire with ground, either 10-2 or 12-2) that reaches comfortably from the disconnect to your new shallow well jet pump. There is a "line" and a "load" side of the disconnect. Attach the wires that will run to the new pump to the "load" side.

Now, remove the cover to the pressure switch on the pump. Ponder it a moment. Notice that a wealth of information is printed on the inside of the cover, like a little schematic of the screws and "device adjustment" advice. As for the mechanics of the switch itself, it's nothing more mysterious than just a couple of wires and a few screws, right? Nothing an adult without a serious drinking problem can't handle. (If you're using the Grundfos MQ and you've read this far anyway, you are excused from pressure-switch-pondering since there is no pressure switch—just a nice, modern push-button control panel.)

Most dual voltage motors come factory wired for 230 volt operation. (230 volts is the same as what we once called 220 volts; 115 volts is the same as 110 volts.) If you have the available power to run the motor as it's wired, do so. It will run more efficiently. If for some reason, your existing well pump is wired for 115 volts, you can convert the rainwater pump to 115 volts by reconnecting the wires as directed by your pump's owner's manual.

Before connecting the wire from the AC disconnect to your new pump's pressure switch, it's a good idea to run the wires

likely the power is directly wired to the control box on the deep well pump or the pressure switch by the existing bladder tank. If either of the latter is the case, mount two AC disconnects to the wall. If you've run fresh wire out to your virgin well site or new pump house, just attach one AC disconnect to the wall.

Now before you do anything else, turn off the power! That means going to your house or power pole—wherever the main breaker box is—and flipping the appropriate breaker to "off" and then making double sure the wire you'll be working with is no longer hot. Don't check it with your tongue. Use one of those cute little voltage testers, the simple one that lights up if you've got power and doesn't light up if you don't. When in doubt, turn all the breakers off. Oh, sure you may have to reset the clocks on the VCR, but at least you'll live to complain about it.

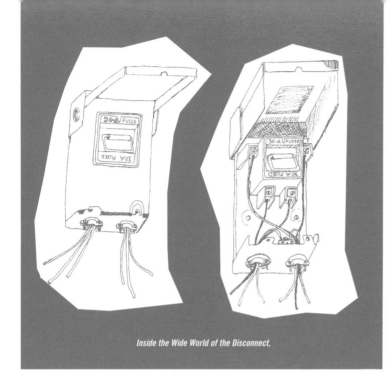

Inside the Wide World of the Disconnect,

GROUND or GRD. Or the screw may be painted green. The power supply wires will go to the two empty terminal screws. The diagram on the inside of the pressure switch cover usually identifies them as "line in" or L1 and L2.)

If you're using an existing power source, disconnect the power supply wire from the old well pump or from the control box or the pressure switch on the existing bladder tank—wherever that thing is. It should not be hot! You did turn off the breaker, right? Check it.

Run power into the disconnect box that your new pump is not connected to. Attach the black wire to one of the "line" terminals and attach the white wire to the other "line" terminal. Then run a length of wire from those same terminals to the "line" terminals in the other disconnect, the one your new pump is connected to. "But, but..." you stutter, scratching your head, "Won't both my well pump and my new rainwater pump come on at the same time if they both are operating on the same circuit (which I did turn off before I began my work)?"

Yep, they will. But if you've installed ball valves in the supply line like we discussed in the final paragraph of the previous section, turning those valves off or on will be how you will regulate your water source.

If you aren't using an existing power source, simply hook the new wire you've run from your breaker box to the "line" side of your one AC disconnect.

It's almost show time. But before the curtain rises, you must first make sure your pump is primed. If it's lower than the water level in your tanks (we're assuming you've collected some rainwater in the time it's taken you to hook everything up), simply

through a "cord strain reliever," a little gizmo available at most hardware stores that makes it more difficult to accidentally pull the wires loose from the screws. It will also prevent the wires from rubbing and wearing against the sharp edges of the hole on the side of the pressure switch housing.

Consult your owner's manual to determine which terminals (they look like screws) to connect your black and white power supply wires to and where to connect the ground wire. It's easy to figure out; the ground goes to the screw that's marked

Double Disconnect for Rainwater and Well Water

Now it's time to pull out the disconnect or fuse handle—in both AC disconnect boxes if you installed two and in one if you installed one. (That's the trouble with how-to manuals: how simplistically can they be written without the simplicity becoming a complication in itself?) Then trot back to the main breaker box and flip the breaker back on and then trot back to the pump and push in the disconnect for the new rainwater pump. As long as you're trotting around, you might as well go open the faucet that's farthest away from the pump so that you can discharge the air in the line.

Leave the disconnect pulled out on the old well pump. Hopefully you'll never have to use it and it will seize up in the "off" position. Hold your tongue right and your pump should whir into action and start filling the pressure tank. Now, open the rest of the ball valves and listen while the rainwater gushes through your pipes and fills up your filter housings. When the pump reaches the preset pressure cut off— usually around 50 psi—it will stop. (Don't forget to go turn that faucet off, though.)

open up that ball valve we had you install between the pump and the tank and let the water run into the pump. (Leave all other ball valves installed in-line after the pump in the "off" position for the time being.)

You can check to make sure the pump is primed by removing the plug in the impeller housing and seeing if water runs out. (Be sure to put the plug back in.)If for some reason you have to manually prime the pump head, refer to the directions that came with your pump. They explain the priming process better than we ever could.

And that's it. You're ready for the freshest, softest shower in your life.

Chapter 7

Tips and Troubleshooting

Chapter 7 Tips and Troubleshooting

L ET'S HOPE YOUR SYSTEM RUNS flawlessly forever and you can completely ignore this chapter. (While we're dreaming, let's also hope for universal peace and the demise of taxes.) But if you should be a mere mortal living in the same challenging world as the rest of us, we're going to share some tips and troubleshooting solutions that we've learned over the years (and years and years), such as how to:

- track down leaks in both the suction or intake line and the pressurized household line.
- determine why your pump won't go on, why you don't have water pressure even if your pump is working, and why your pump won't go off.
- figure out why your collection tanks aren't filling even though it's raining, why you can't unscrew the filter housings, and why your shower fixtures are green.
- prepare for the big chill and wage a personal war on mosquitoes.

Sneaky Leaks

When plumbing was invented, the word "leak" took on much more ominous meanings. One of the biggest challenges you face as a self-reliant operator of a personal water system is leakage, either during the initial start-up of your system or as time, weather, and marauding hoof stock take their toll on defenseless piping and pumps.

Drop By Drop

So you think a leak is just a drop in the bucket? Then just consider how those drips add up:

30 drops/minute = 54 gallons/month = 648 gallons/year
60 drops/minute = 113 gallons/month = 1356 gallons/year
120 drops/minute = 237 gallons/month = 2844 gallons/year

When Leaks Suck

The first clue that you have a leak on the suction side of your pump (in the line between the pump and the collection tank) is that your pump won't turn off, yet still has trouble building up enough pressure. Or the pump will discharge at full steam and then fail. Or it might deliver a trickle or nothing at all. Since a pump wants to suck pure water—no air, no dirt, no leaves—even a pinhole leak on the suction side of the line will give your pump fits.

To check for a leak, first shut the ball valve at the outlet of the collection tank. Next, disconnect the nice flexible stainless steel tubing we suggested that you attach to the suction port of the pump. (See, we told you it would come in handy.) Bend it up so that you can pour water in it. Fill the line with water. (It may take some patience because you're forcing out the air in the tube with water.) Once the line is full, wander off for a couple of hours, then check the line to see if the water has dropped. If it has, you obviously have a leak. You must find it and fix it.

Now, here's the most depressing aspect of a suction-side leak: even if you perform the previous test and the water level doesn't visibly drop, you may still have a miniscule, but troublesome leak. You can first try the old shaving cream trick to find it. With the system turned off, just squirt some of the foamy stuff on a joint or fitting that you suspect of leaking. Turn on the system and—voila—the shaving cream will be sucked into the pipe wherever there's a leak.

Sometimes a leak can only be detected using pressurized air. If this is the case, you'll need to head to the hardware or plumbing store to snag yourself a "pressure test gauge", a fancy name for a brass plumbing fitting equipped with a pressure gauge and a shrader valve (like the valve stem on your bicycle or car tires). This is the doohickey that plumbers attach to the household water lines so they can use the shrader valve to pump the lines full of air and check for leaks by watching the needle on the gauge. Now, lucky you, you get to use a pressure test gauge the very same way.

Start by shutting the ball valve at the outlet of your collection tank and the ball valve you installed (right?) between the pump discharge line and the filter housings. Next, cut into your suction or intake line between your collection tank and the pump. Glue in the appropriate sized "tee" and then reduce its outlet if needed to fit a 3/4-inch threaded nipple. Screw in the pressure test gauge, making certain to use a little Teflon tape or plumber's goop. (That's all you need to do—create a leak when you're trying to find a leak.) Use a bicycle pump or air compressor to charge the line. Do not exceed 30 psi. If the gauge drops, you've got a leak. Sometimes by pressurizing the line with air, you can locate the leak by following your ears. (The air and the little remaining water in the line will sometime produce a nice gurgling hiss.)

When the Pressure Is On

If you have a leak in your household water supply lines, you can look forward to investigating a host of suspects, from something as apparent as a dripping filter housing that's missing an O-ring to a nefarious leak in the plumbing buried in deep in your slab.

The most common culprit when it comes to leaks is the toilet. You can often hear the leak by putting your ear to the side of the tank. (Make certain no one catches you doing this.) If you can hear the water leaking out (i.e. the toilet is "running"), you could be losing up to 200 gallons of water a day! If you hear nothing, this doesn't mean you're in the clear. You can test for silent leaks by dropping a dye tablet or a few drops of red or blue or green (never yellow) food coloring into the toilet tank. Now, don't flush it! If the dye seeps from the tank into the bowl, you've caught your thief. You can also test your toilet by shutting off its water supply line and seeing if the level of water in the tank drops over time.

To arrest this aquatic hooligan, you may need to simply adjust the float ball or replace the flapper ball or throw your hands up in the air and call a plumber (or at least go to the library and check out a good book on plumbing repairs.)

If the toilet is innocent, expand your investigation.

First check the usual (and easy to inspect) suspects, like all along any exposed pressured line, especially at vulnerable joints and where the pipe joins components like pumps, bladder tanks, filter housings, etc.

Still no culprit? He might be in hiding. Do you have a pressure gauge installed in-line at your pump or filter housings? If so, you can trace a possible leak by keeping an eye on this gauge. First, make sure that no water is being used in the house (Did you remember to turn off the valve to the icemaker and the reverse osmosis unit under the sink?) If the pressure reading on the gauge drops, even though no water is being used, you've got a leak.

But identifying the culprit doesn't mean he'll be easy to catch. Finding the leak now, whether it's in the wall, the ground, or the slab is a frustrating process of trial and error. As a last resort, you may have to call one of those high tech plumbing outfits who've purchased all the latest gadgetry, including a leak detector that

uses sonar to track the sound of running water.

The Voice of Experience

One summer during an extended dry spell, we noticed—first with mystification and then with growing horror—that the water level in our tank was dropping faster than dot com stocks in 2000. We checked all the toilets; they were behaving themselves perfectly. Making certain we weren't using any water in the house, we monitored the flow meter we'd installed in-line after the filter housings and calculated a water loss of more than 50 gallons a day!

After much stomping around, thumping of pipes, and randomly smashing holes in the Sheetrock walls, we finally determined that the leak was somewhere in the master bathroom. (We could actually hear the water "running" when we put our ear to the wall.) We also determined that it was the hot water line, so we were not only wasting water but propane as well! (In one of those spiteful hindsight epiphanies, we suddenly realized why we hadn't had to run the hot water in our shower for very long before it was hot, even though the water heater was a good sixty feet away—because the hot water was always running!)

We smashed some more arbitrary holes in the walls (warning:

it's much more fun to smash them than repair them) then finally called a plumbing company who brought out their cool sonar gizmo and—for a mere $250!—detected the leak in the slab of the bathroom floor. Now we knew we had a leak and we knew where it was and we'd thrown some money (and some fits) at the problem, but we still hadn't solved it. After prolonged procrastination, we finally decided to disconnect the hot water line running to the bathroom (we found a place to perform this operation in a manifold in the kitchen wall below the sink) and install another water heater in the master bathroom using the still viable cold water line.

The Mandatory How-to-Book Q & A Session

My pump won't go on! Do I have to move back to the city?

Not necessarily, but if you don't quit whining that might be the best place for a sissy like you.

- Check the obvious first: Is your pump plugged in or switched on? Is a breaker tripped? Are any wires loose or disconnected at the pressure switch or pump motor?
- The pressure switch contacts may be dirty and stuck shut. Clean pressure switch contacts with a fine emery cloth. Or the pressure switch may be literally bugged—by fire ants. These little devils can be attracted to electrical currents (maybe that's how they recharge their stingers) and if a lot of these thrill-seekingHymenoptera pile up on a electrical device, they will short it out. Check the pressure switch and clean out all the little bodies. Worst case scenario: You may have to replace the pressure switch.
- The pump impeller may be jammed or clogged. Your clue to this is to listen to see if the pump is humming. (It will be an aimless

unidentifiable song.)

If the pump is hot to the touch, it could have simply over heated because the pump impeller or diffuser is biting the dust and the automatic thermal protection thing-a-ma-bob (it's inside a thermally protected motor) has shut the pump off. It needs to cool down and then it will reset itself and restart. If it continues to happen, you may need to replace the impeller and diffuser. (Whenever you replace the impeller, you might as well replace the diffuser.) Or the impeller/diffuser might be fine and instead your check valve may be stuck shut. (See the following for a long-winded explanation on how to diagnose and medicate a sick check valve.)

I don't have any water pressure! Who do I sue?

- Yourself? You probably need to change your filthy filters.
- There may air trapped in the pump or the suction line. Try repriming the pump.
- You may need to increase the pressure by turning the appropriate screw on the pump's pressure switch clockwise. (Check pump manual for directions.) Turn the screw one revolution at a time and test the pressure between turns. You may have to increase the pressure in your bladder tank accordingly.
- The problem might be in the check valve, which can be very intolerant to grit and debris that can cause it to stick open. (This is yet another argument for pre-filtering the water before it enters the tank.) And a check valve, as simple as it is, can also occasionally malfunction, with the spring, the valve or the seat simply failing. If either debris or check valve failure is to blame, the pump will cycle off and on rapidly or it will be

running continuously without building pressure. Without a properly functioning check valve, the water is being pulled into the pump from the tank and then pushed back into the tank. Sometimes you can determine if this is happening by looking through the manway into the collection tank and seeing the water being pushed back into it. You might even see bubbles by the suction port of the pump.

What should you do? First, try tapping or banging on the check valve. (Really. You might be able to dislodge any crud that's hampering the valve with a Fonzie-like blow.) If this fails to work, you'll have to remove the check valve. Hold it upright like a little cup with the arrow pointing up. Pour water into the top. If water pours out the bottom, you've discovered the problem. Using a little brush or a toughened finger, clean around the valve where it meets the seat. When it's spic and span, check it again. If the water still pours out, fling that check valve as far away as you can and install a nice fresh one.

- The impeller/diffuser in the pump may be worn out. Replace it according to the pump manufacturer's instructions.
- The pump venturi—a narrow tube through which water is force and yet another replaceable part in a jet pump—may be plugged by debris. Remove and clean.

My pump never goes off or it goes on and off rapidly! Do I have to sell my house and move?

- Probably not. If you don't have a leak, the pump's most fragile parts—the impeller or diffuser or venturi or injector—have given up the fight. Rebuild the pump. (And don't forget

to replace the seal. It's one of those things: "As long as I'm going to do all this stuff, I might as well replace the seal.")

- If this occurs during the initial start up—and you are certain that the pump is primed—you may have exceeded the lift capacity of the pump. Rethink your setup. (Remember: most shallow-well jet pumps can lift water no father than 23 feet or so.)
- The problem could be that you haven't set the pressure on your bladder tank to two pounds below the cut-on pressure of your pump. There's a chart on the inside of the cover to the pressure switch with the cut-in and cut-out pressure. Typically, it's 30-50 psi or maybe 40-60 psi. The pressure in your bladder tank should be set to 2 psi below the cut-in pressure of the pump (28 psi or 38 psi respectively). You determine the pressure setting of your bladder tank by draining it of water and checking the pressure at the shrader valve on top of it, using nothing more sophisticated than a tire gauge.
- If your pressure is properly set and the pump still misbehaves, check out the check valve that you put between the suction side of the pump and the tank. (You did put one there, didn't you?) See procedure for inspecting the check valve in answers to previous question.
- You might also have a leak in the suction line on the pump. (See When Leaks Suck above.)

We had a huge rain and my tank is only half full!!! Has my tank sprung a leak?!
Maybe, but probably not.

- Have you tried cleaning your gutters? You'd be surprised how often this is the problem. Remember to install some sort of screen in your gutters at the downspouts: 1/4 - inch hardware cloth is great but at the very least use some chicken (a.k.a squirrel) wire to keep the bushy-tailed rodents out of your downpipes and trunklines.

- You could possibly have a clog in your trunk line. (Just hope it's not a squirrel.) To check for a clog, make sure your trunk lines are full of water and then systematically open all your drain valves one by one, beginning with the one at the lowest elevation. The water should gush out. If it doesn't, you'll need to locate the clog and cut it out. It will most likely be where a downpipe makes a 90-degree turn to meet the trunk line. And if you think this through logically before you start sawing up your trunkline, you'll realize that the obstruction is most likely to occur where you have the highest leaf drop. If you're smart—and we know you are because you bought this book—once you discover the kink in the works, you'll install a clean-out (one of those fittings with a cap you can unscrew and reach in and "clean out" the pipe) at this clog-vulnerable spot.
- Make sure the air vents in your tank are open.
- Make sure any drains on your trunk lines are shut. (Of course, you would never forget to shut them, but maybe someone else has tampered with them.)
- If you have a roof washer, make certain the drain is shut on that as well. Or could it possibly need cleaning? (On more than one occasion, we've received frantic calls from customers who have so neglected their roof washers that the filter acts more like a plug than a filter.)
- Or did you forget to close the valve on your site indicator? One irate woman thought her tank was leaking. It turned out

she had left the valve open on the site indicator and the water had leaked out of the tank via the site indicator tubing. Her excess tubing hung over the tank's inlet and then draped about halfway back down her tank. This created a siphon and, while she was on vacation, the water drained out until it leveled off in the tank even with the end of the tube.

What is all this stuff in my water??!! Is my tank shedding?

No. If you've switched from well water to rainwater, it's probably all the calcium that's built up in your pipes being released by the slightly acidic rainwater. It's nothing time won't cure. We get calls from people who are upset that their sediment filters are dirty after a month. We try to explain to them as gently as possible that a dirty filter is a filter that's doing its job—and maybe it's time to change the filter!

Note: An activated charcoal filter can get shaken up during shipping and when this shook-up filter is slipped into the housing, it can briefly make your tap water look gray and foamy. (How briefly? Like a couple of gallons worth.) While this gray and foamy and gross-looking water isn't harmful, some manufacturers recommend that you first rinse a new activated charcoal filter in warm water prior to installing it.

I can't get the filter housings unscrewed!!

Remember to take your vitamins? Eat your spinach? Hold your tongue right?

Actually, the problem is probably caused by pressure in the housings. Be sure to close off the ball valve before the filter and to push the pressure relief button on the top of the housing until no air or water squirts out. When you finally get them off, lubricate the O-rings with plumber's grease.

Why are my shower faucets and shower tiles green?

Ah, now we must confess to one of rainwater's less agreeable characteristics: its aggression towards untreated metals, like your copper pipes, the source of your green build-up. (This aggressive quality towards metals is a strong argument for using the newer plastic piping we discussed in Chapter 6, especially if you're building a new house.)

Water is either corrosive, scale forming, or stable. The stable range, unfortunately, is relatively narrow, and determined by a number of factors, usch as pH, hardness, total alkalinity, temperature, flow velocity, piping material, and possibly the phases of the moon. (Just kidding about the moon.) Entire books have been published on the subject. We do not want to write a book or even many paragraphs on the subject, especially since the National Association of Corrosion Engineers has claimed that "Essentially no statement regarding corrosion on the use of a material can be made that does not have an exception." Great.

Some of rainwater's finest qualities—like a hardness of zero and its slight acidity courtesy of the carbon dioxide it collects in the atmosphere—are the very catalysts for its corrosive nature. Rainwater also has very little alkalinity. So, the upshot is— rainwater can eat your pipes.

The simplest and most effective way to address the problem is to adjust the pH of your rainwater. The addition of soda ash (sodium carbonate) to the rainwater will raise your pH. Some experts may suggests that water also needs some hardness to help

prevent corrosion. You can increase the hardness of the rainwater by adding calcium carbonate.

Wonder what's the point of collecting soft rainwater if you have to harden it? You're not alone. Personally, we'd rather suffer a little corrosion rather than add hardness to our rainwater. To quote a paper we read on the Wilkes University website, "Corrosion control is a complex science, requiring considerable knowledge of corrosion chemistry and of the system being evaluated." Unless you're prepared to study such things as the Langelier Saturation Index (SI=pH-pHs)—considered by the American Water Works Association to be "the most widely used and misused index in the water treatment and distribution field"—we say get your water tested if you're worried (especially if you have very old pipes and there's a chance of lead solder lurking there). Otherwise, simply check the pH, add a bit of soda ash from time to time, and enjoy your soft rainwater. As rainwater guru Mike McElveen says: "Corrosion isn't a rainwater problem; it's a plumbing problem."

Frost Bit

When it's warm and rainy, it's easy to love your collection system. But when it freezes, you are roughly reminded that independence and responsibility go hand-in-hand. When water freezes, its volume increases by eleven percent. This is more than enough expansion to shatter your pipes, your pump and your patience. (Dripping your faucets is not an option in the rainwater world, unless you set up some kind of recirculating system so that you don't lose a drop of your finite supply.)

Ideally, your outdoor plumbing should all slope gradually

down to the lowest spot, where you can install a central drain. Barring this ideal setup, you can put a drain at all the lowest points. Every system is different and so, each comes with

surprise idiosyncrasies during a freeze, things you can't believe you didn't anticipate. We discovered some of our weak arctic links after a freezing rain fell on our roof and the standing water in our downpipes froze. The water on the roof thawed before the water in the down pipes thawed. All that precious water filled the gutters and then overflowed onto the ground.

So think about a way to drain your downpipes if they're lower than your tank inlet, and thus, are filled with water waiting to freeze. Another solution to this problem would be to circulate water through the gutter system via a garden hose at a fast enough rate to prevent it from freezing.

You'll also want to protect any equipment not located in your toasty main house. In our area, a 100-watt light bulb usually generates enough heat in a small pump house to protect pipes and pumps. If you anticipate an extreme freeze headed your way or you can't protect your equipment for some reason, you may want to simply shut your system down entirely by unplugging the pump, draining all your lines, and heading for Tobago until spring.

Before you go, however, you must not forget to drain the pump itself, yet another lesson we learned the frozen way. If only we had unscrewed the little plug on the lower part of the pump's impeller housing, we wouldn't have returned home to a cracked pump.

Despite these experiences, we have to admit that since we live well below the reach of prolonged winters, our practical knowledge of freeze-induced dilemmas is very limited. (Coincidentally, as we write this in February of 2003, an arctic blast has brought our typically balmy region a couple of inches of ice and two days of below freezing temps, completely shutting down highways, schools, and mail service. Wrecked and abandoned cars litter the highway as though it's the Day After. During this record cold snap, we received calls from a couple of clients who were experiencing more rapid build-up on their 5-micron sediment filters than normal. The only cause for this increase in gunk that we could come up with was that the water in their tanks was "turning over"— inversion, we think they call it—and stirring up sediments from the bottom of the tank.)

To our northern buddies, we can offer sympathy and general advice like installing tank heaters and such, but we have no respectable experiences to back up this advice. For this, we highly recommend Max Burn's colorfully written and illustrated book *Cottage Water Systems*. (See appendix.) It addresses, in detail, the plumbing concerns—from drinking water systems to outhouses—of folks who own cottages in the Canadian hinterlands.

Just an idea: We do understand that the freeze problem extends even beyond the formidable tasks of keeping your tanks and plumbing from freezing. We've heard about the problems that gutters and ice dams create. Why, even right here in Central Texas during the arctic blast, one of our clients watched as the giant sheet of ice that had formed on his metal roof slid off en masse and ripped the gutters right off the house. We have a suggestion for a solution to this, inspired by none other than a presidential residence built here in North Central Texas a few years ago. Of course, we've never seen the actual home (guess our invitation was lost in the mail) but we did see the architectural plans for the Crawford house.

The rainwater was collected off the roof, not into gutters, but into a gravel-filled trough that ran just below the drip line along the perimeter of the house. If memory serves (and it often doesn't), this trough system—wherein the gravel served as a crude filter—drained to a pond or—as we call them here in Texas—a stock tank. We don't know if this rainwater was simply collected for irrigation purposes or if it was to be treated for household use, but it struck us that in the right circumstances, this might the answer to the destructive combination of gutters and ice.

When Buzz is Bad

What we lack in experience dealing with hard freezes, we more than make up for with our experience dealing with mosquitoes. So does this mean we know how to easily eliminate the little bloodsuckers? Of course not. We have learned what doesn't work. Take those black light mosquito zappers. One can electrocute thousands of insects, including many beneficial bugs, in a 24-hour period, but, on average, mosquitoes make up only around six percent of the death toll. And only half of those mosquitoes killed are bloodthirsty females. And while we love bats and purple martins and certainly acknowledge their many benefits, we've learned that these creatures' effects on mosquito populations are minimal. We also know that we certainly aren't going to soak our property with pesticides and that even adding biological controls like Bacillus thruingiensis 'Israelensis' to our household water supply is a big no-no.

In theory, the solution to the mosquito problem seems easy enough: eliminate standing water and you'll eliminate the nurseries that mosquito larvae require to grow into big, obnoxious disease carrying creeps. In practice, however, this solution requires near obsessive attention to such things as cleaning gutters, draining downpipes completely between rain events during skeeter season,

How to Put a Drain Anywhere

If the trunk line from your gutters to your storage tank will be holding water, you may want to prepare for a freeze by putting a drain at the lowest point(s). With any luck, there will be a coupling at or near this point; it's nice to tap into an area of "double strength" PVC where pipe and coupling meet. Using a new, sharp 1½-inch paddle bit, drill through one side (not all the way through both sides!) of the pipe halfway up the side. (Or less than halfway, the point being you want to drill at the lowest point without grinding through the dirt to do so.)

Next, take a National pipe thread tap and screw it into the hole. This cuts the threads for the 1/2-inch hosebib you'll next screw into the hole. Be sure to use a little Teflon tape or plumber's gunk and be sure to keep the faucet turned off except when you're draining your lines before a big freeze or if you're battling mosquitoes by eliminating standing water.

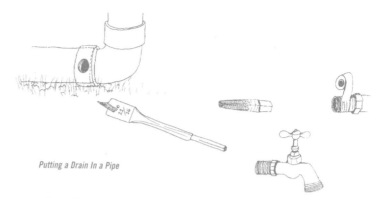

Putting a Drain In a Pipe

screening all tank vents, and draining the roof washer. If you have an Eliminator, you'll need to monitor it for breeding activity and drain it accordingly.

We are currently experimenting with installing a flapper-style check valve in the vertical section of the trunkline just prior to the inlet of the Eliminator. We hope that this will seal in any mosquitoes that might wash into the Eliminator or your collection tanks where they can only bug one another until they die. Or be sucked into the pump where they will be ground up and filtered out through your 5-micron sediment/mosquito pulp filter.

And in all your spare time, you must sit and think like a mosquito. (Don't act like one, just think like one.) So it might help—or not—to know that some species of mosquitoes lay up to 300 eggs at one time and that, depending on temperature, these eggs can mature into adults in as little as a week. Hauntingly, eggs can even be laid in a dry environment (your clean gutters) where they can remain for weeks or months, waiting until they are covered with water to hatch.

So, what's your summer mantra? No standing water, no standing water, no standing...

Appendix Information, Please

Alternative Energy Sourcebook, 7th Edition, Edited by John Schaeffer, Real Goods Trading Corporation, 13771 S. Highway 101 Hopland, CA 95449, 800-919-2400, 707-744-2100. www.realgoods.com

We put in a system for a family's remote cottage that relied on a solar panel and 12-volt battery for pumping power. If you're inclined to "live off the grid", Real Goods Trading Corporation (now merged with Jade Mountain and a part of Gaiam) offers a complete line of products for energy independence. And best of all, they happily offer technical advice to go along with their products.

Cottage Water Systems, Max Burns, 1995, Cottage Life Books, 111 Queen St. E., Ste. 408, Toronto, Ontario, Canada, M5C 1S2 or Cottage Life Inc., Box 1338, Ellicott Station, Buffalo, NY, 14205.

Those cold winters give our neighbors to the north a great sense of humor, even about a topic as alternately dull and complicated as water systems. While there is little on rainwater collection specifically, Burns offers a wealth of easily understood information about water treatment, pumps and plumbing. The chapter on outhouses alone is worth the price of admission. Great graphics.

Drinking Water, Refreshing Answers to All Your Questions, James M. Symons, 1995, Texas A&M University Press.

The author answers 128 water-related questions on everything from "Is tap water suitable for use in a home kidney dialysis machine?" to "What makes ice cubes cloudy?" We especially like the water-related quotes proceeding each chapter.

The Drinking Water Book, A Complete Guide to Safe Drinking Water, Colin Ingram, 1995, Ten Speed Press, P.O. Box 7123, Berkeley CA, 94707.

It's a bit too doomful and we don't agree with all of Mr. Ingram's conclusions, but the book is noteworthy for its Consumer-Reports-style rating of equipment like filters and disinfection units.

The Home Water Supply: How to Find Filter, Store, and Conserve It, Stu Campbell, 1983, A Garden Way Publishing Book, Storey Communications, Inc, Pownal, Vermont, 05261.

A very comprehensive tome about getting yourself supplied with water. Mostly concerned with surface water—a lake or pond or river—as your source, but lots of information about pumping, treatment, testing, etc. applies equally to rainwater collection.

Sustainable Building Sourcebook. Compiled by the City of Austin's Green Builder Program, this online compendium provides information about green building practices—from strawbale construction to gray water irrigation systems. http://www.greenbuilder.com/sourcebook.

Texas Guide to Rainwater Harvesting, Texas Water Development Board in Cooperation with the Center for Maximum Potential Building Systems, P.O. Box 13231, 512/463-7847.

A booklet whose best features are the rather inspirational case studies listed in back and whose worse features are its complicated formulas for determining water needs and the amount of rain you can collect. You can even download an electronic version at www.twdb.state.tx.us/publications/reports/RainHarv.pdf

The Water We Drink, Joshua I. Barzilay, M.D., Winkler G. Weinberg, M.D., and J. William Eley, M.D., 2000, Rutgers University Press, 100 Joyce Kilmer Avenue, Piscataway, NJ 08854-8099.

Not much in here about rainwater collection, but a very intriguing treatise on drinking water, its history, and its effects on our health. Exhaustive bibliography of articles from medical textbooks and journals.

Organizations

American Rainwater Catchment Systems Association
P.O. Box 12521, Austin, TX 78711-2521, www.arcsa-usa.org
Downloads available of a variety of papers on topics related to rainwater collection and information about central Texas rainwater collection business.

Center For Maximum Potential Building Systems
8604 FM 969, Austin, TX 78724 512.928.4786, www.cmpbs.org.
This non-profit organization helped co-author the Texas Guide to Rainwater Harvesting. They're a great source for information on innovative sustainable building techniques that they've experimented with over the last two decades.

International Rainwater Catchment Systems Association
www.ircsa.org
This organization promotes rainwater collection worldwide. The website offers information about projects ranging from micro-catchment dams in Brazil to ancient Mexican cisterns.

The Olive Branch
P.O. Box 1421, Lawrenceville, GA 30046,
www.theolivebranch.com
Loads of online information—including some very scary statistics—about water contamination and safety.

Acknowledgements

Our deepest appreciation to John and
Beth Weinstock, who jumped on board when the boat
was still rocking ; the inspiring duo of Mike and Kathy
McElveen, who went forth into the land of rainwater
collection where no persons had gone in a long time;
Bill Goodwin for all his helpful insights; Harley and Patty
Clark for bailing us out of trouble; and Trent Shepherd, of
Cold Shower Design for designing our website.

Index

Raindrops are not tear-shaped. Depending on size, they can be spherical or shaped like a kidney bean.

Rainwater Collection for the Mechanically Challenged

Trying to figure out how much this will cost? Visit www.rainwatercollection.com for current prices.

NOTES

How many gallons of water can you collect
in a year? Remember this easy formula: Take the
square footage of your collection surface, divide
by 1000, multiply by 550, then multiply by your
average annual rainfall in inches.

Rainwater Collection for the Mechanically Challenged